NO GRAVEN IMAGE

No Graven Image

A NOVEL BY
ELISABETH ELLIOT

CROSSWAY BOOKS • WESTCHESTER, ILLINOIS
A DIVISION OF GOOD NEWS PUBLISHERS

TO TOM,
my brother, who is also
my friend

First printing, 1982.
Second printing, 1982.
Third printing, 1983.
Fourth printing, 1985.

Cover illustration and design: Britt Taylor Collins

Printed in the United States of America.

Library of Congress Catalog Card Number 81-71346

ISBN 0-89107-235-7

FOREWORD
by J. I. Packer

When would-be writers ask me for advice on fulfilling their ambition, I warn them that there is more to it than Enid Blyton's formula, going broody over a typewriter, might suggest. I tell them there are three essentials: first, something to say, something you have seen and want to share; second, enough technique to enable it to find its own best shape on paper; third, a strong bottom on which you can sit for hours together handcrafting sentences, paragraphs, and chapters. Sometimes my advice stops folk in their tracks. How much real wisdom it contains others must judge; I only know that this is what has come home to me during twenty-five years of trying to write myself. I judge, however, from the vivid, economical, fastidious Anglo-Saxon which fills Elisabeth Elliot's shrewd and shapely books that she, at least, is a member of my club.

No Graven Image is a novel that grew out of personal missionary experience of which she has written elsewhere, notably in *These Strange Ashes*, *The Savage My Kinsman*, *The Liberty of Obedience* and a haunting article, "The Wake," in the March 1964 issue of *Eternity*. I suppose she turned from biography, autobiography, and essays to the novel form (i.e., an imagined story of people in relationship against a chosen background of scenes and events) because it was most apt for what she had to say. Certainly, the sense of significance for the reader which a good novelist evokes by rousing him to imaginative involvement in the story is more than nonfictional analysis can ever convey. (Thus, if you want to feel the force of Tolstoy's view of Christianity, you read, not *What I Believe*, but his novel, *Resurrection*.) *No Graven Image* shows its author to be a pretty good novelist, and anyone who can identify with her narrator's state of mind depicted in the opening chapters will find the story dynamite.

Christian novelists today have a hard furrow to plough. The secular world finds their vision of life unconvincing, and the Christian world lacks interest in their attempts to express that vision in their stories. Part of the trouble here is the prevalence of a different type of Christian fiction, stemming from the "edifying" tracts and children's stories of the last century, having the nature not of novels but of sermons. As musical comedies tend to embody what P. G. Wodehouse called the oldest plot in the world, boy meets girl—boy loses girl—boy gets girl, so this type of Christian fiction is usually built round a two-pronged plot formula, someone turns from God and finds trouble—someone in trouble turns to God and is blessed. Unhappily, these moral tales, though not novels, often claim this name, and so spread the idea that this is what "real" Christian novels are like. The result, both funny and sad, is that when folk fed on this diet read a genuine novel by a Christian novelist (Graham Greene, say, or Charles Williams, or George Target, or Flannery O'Connor, or Fyodor Dostoevski, or Aleksandr Solzhenitsyn) their appreciation, if any, is overshadowed by regret and puzzlement that the author did not so manipulate his characters as to produce a straightforward moral tale, clearly illustrating the gospel. No suspicion that the novel is a different thing from the moral tale enters their heads.

What, then, is the novelist's task? Karl Barth, who though no literary critic was a Christian, a reader, a thinker and very much a modern man, answered the question thus: "I expect him [the novelist] to show me man as he always is in the man of today, my contemporary... I expect the novel to give evidence on every page that its author not only knows this man (his character) properly and sees right through him, from the depths of his heart to his outward manners and mode of speaking, but also treats him honestly, i.e., loves him as he is and as he is not, without regret or contempt. Furthermore, it should tell me what its author finds special in this man—that and no more. In other words, it should have no plans for educating me, but should leave me to reflect (or not) on the basis of the portrait with which I am presented. Finally, its form should correspond to the portrait of the man whom it presents; its form should be necessary, strict and impressive to the extent that I do not forget the man I have been shown in his temporal and timeless aspects. I should be able to live with him, and indeed perhaps have to live with him, again and again" (quoted in E. Busch, *Karl Barth*, p.313). On this showing, Barth would have recognized *No Graven Image* as a true novel, just as he would have recognized its vision of God's sovereign freedom as a truth of biblical faith.

When the book first appeared in the USA, some took it as expressing disillusionment with evangelical missionary endeavor as such, and were offended. But this is clearly not its thrust, even though for the sake of the story some cultural aspects of that endeavor get guyed in a way which they might be thought to deserve. *No Graven Image* is not bitter or resentful (in fact, patient good-will suffuses it throughout). It is a simple story about knowing God, or (which is really the same thing) the growth of a soul, and the place where the action happens is in the narrator's mind. She starts as the victim of a well-meant, God-shrinking, success-oriented notion of the "work" (Christian work, missionary work, God's work, my work) which fills her with zany confidence but keeps her from realism about either herself or her God. By the end of the book she knows what the authors of Job and Ecclesiastes taught—that God's providence is inscrutable, that apparent tragedy, frustration and waste are the lot of God's servants no less than of other men (perhaps, indeed, more), that God exalts himself by putting us down, and that it is not for us to claim to see the meaning of all that happens. Learning this leaves her an outsider, no longer able to identify with the phony streak in what she embraced before; but in not identifying she finds herself free, God real, and life good. How powerfully the narrative builds to its climax, and how hauntingly it poses its questions about ends justifying means, results mocking motives, and the value of misguided sincerity, the reader will discover. I must stop, lest I spoil for you a story which will rivet your attention from the start, and at the end blow your mind.

I first read *No Graven Image* ten years ago, and it bowled me over; partly, no doubt, because its vision of God struck so many chords in my own experience. I thought it was a little classic; a miniature maybe, but a gem. Reading it again, this time without the surprise and excitement of unanticipated empathy, I find that I think just the same. I count myself honoured to be asked to commend it to a new generation of readers, and I do so with very great pleasure.

But do please remember—it's a novel; it is not anything else.

I will manifest my holiness among you in the sight of the nations.
And you shall know that I am the Lord.

And I shall be profaned through you in the sight of the nations;
And you shall know that I am the Lord.

And her prophets have daubed for them with whitewash, seeing
false visions and divining lies for them, saying, "Thus says the
Lord God," when the Lord has not spoken.

Ezekiel 20:41, 42; 22:16, 28.

NO GRAVEN IMAGE

CHAPTER

1

INSIDE THE railway car there was a vacuum of stillness which seemed to shut in the passengers, making us acutely conscious of the slightest sound or movement. For no good reason, I was listening, hardly drawing breath. It was not quite six o'clock in the morning. Everyone else was half-asleep and thoroughly chilled, for the sun had not yet risen, but they waited with far more patience than I for the train to begin its journey up into the western cordillera of the Andes and down to the coast. It had been scheduled to leave at half past five, and although I had been in Ecuador long enough to learn to expect delays, I was especially eager to begin the last leg of what had been a very long journey, a whole life's preparation for missionary work among mountain Indians.

The door opened, relieving the vacuum, and a timid voice spoke. "Little suitcases. Toys. One sucre."

A woman in a plaid shawl and long wool skirt came in, steering a basket in front of her between the closely set seats. She saw me as soon as I turned. A foreigner was always a likely customer.

"Only one sucre, señorita." She stopped by my seat, proffering the basket with a look of humility and hope.

One sucre. About five cents. I took one of the tiny valises from the basket. It was made of layers of newspaper, pasted together and covered with an imitation leather paper. There were a little handle and a strap with a gold-colored buckle to fasten it shut. The valise measured perhaps two inches across.

"Did you make it?" I asked.

"*Sí*, señorita. I made it myself."

"But what a lot of work! One sucre, did you say?"

"*Sí*, señorita, one sucre, no more. It is not very expensive, señorita. Look at how nicely it is made. It is very pretty. Just one sucre."

"Oh no, it is not very expensive," I agreed. "I don't see how you can make money on it at all."

"Well, I don't make much, señorita, but it is something. I have six children. I try to care for them. Sometimes my daughter helps me. She is twelve. She can paste the paper for me. Don't you want one, señorita?"

"Yes, I want one." I put the sucre into her hand and took the little suitcase. I would find some child to give it to. An Indian child, perhaps. The MacDonalds, who were to meet me at the end of the train trip, were older. Their children were grown.

It would be nice to be met this time by experienced missionaries, and to stay in their home. My arrival in Guayaquil, six months before, had been quite different. The thin line of shore that I could see when the ship dropped anchor was like a line drawn to mark off a section of my life. When I crossed it, everything would change. The days aboard ship had given me a taste of a world I had never known and would not know again, a world of luxuries such as Camembert cheese, deft waiters, soft music at dinner. Standing on deck during the last moments before disembarking I felt a faint wind stir my hair and I turned to face it, closed my eyes, and tried to see the far-off shore with its palm trees and thatched huts, the brown children running on the sand where the wind came from. It would not be long. Unaccountably, I wished that it would be. The door opened behind me, giving forth the breath of the little world within—cooled air, smelling of perfumes, cigarette smoke, steaks, alcohol. I wanted to prolong, not just indefinitely but forever, those timeless days of the voyage, when I was no longer preparing to be a missionary nor had yet become one. The irresponsibility was intoxicating. Now I would have to cross the line.

I went below and put a few last things into my suitcase. My leather-bound Bible lay on the dresser and I reached toward it for reassurance. "Fear thou not, for I am with thee." The Bible had opened easily at that passage, for it was a favorite of mine and it was to me now the voice of God. I left the ship, and then there had been the trip upriver by launch and my first night in an Ecuadorian hotel, with its smell of plaster, mold, cheap soap and floor wax; the smothering heat, the short bed and unyielding pillow, the sounds of coughing and spitting in the hall, of dogs barking in the streets. A clock had boomed out the hour and the half hour, a mosquito sang his thin song close to my ear, and a trumpet in a nearby dance hall had hooted and shrilled. The place of God's choice for me, I had reflected, so little discomforts, little sacrifices, were to be welcomed.

"Toys, sir? Suitcases, señora? Toys for your children. Only one sucre." The poor woman was back, making another attempt to sell her trinkets. Small chance that anyone in the next car had bought one—it was second class, with long wooden benches facing the center on

[3]

which huddled Indians in ponchos and women with great cloth bundles and baskets. The toy vendor's voice was drowned much of the time by the strident cries of white-aproned women on the platform who were selling plates of cooked food.

In front of me sat a man in a black hat and a dark red poncho, cradling a burlap-wrapped package on his lap; the smell of the damp wool of his poncho was mixed with the heavy sweet smell of brilliantine with which his wife had slicked her black braid. Across the aisle were two men in black suits and black ties, reading newspapers. Three children a little ahead of them had turned one of the seats around to make a cubicle of privacy. With their mother they made a small cosmos, squirming and twisting in the seats as they arranged themselves and their bundles, looking at last with satisfaction at one another. There was no one else in the train, so far as they were concerned. Yes, there was. One of them spied me. Three other faces turned toward me. *La gringa!* Look at the *gringuita!* There was that word again—the foreigner—but I was used to it now. I had heard it a hundred times in the streets of Guayaquil, and later in Ambato, where I studied Spanish. They turned back and looked solemnly at their mother as though their security had been jeopardized. The two who faced me shifted their eyes quickly toward me now and then, and I tried to meet their glances with a smile. I wouldn't hurt you. Really, I am not dangerous, even if I am a *gringa.* They pretended they hadn't seen.

"Eggs! Fresh-cooked eggs!" A woman stuck her head in the car, and behind her another pushed in and shrieked, "Eggs! Potatoes! Tender corn!"

A whistle screamed, the train suddenly hissed and jerked, the two vendors lurched against the doorway and

[4]

scrambled for the platform. Poor things! How much could they make in that business? I looked out the window and saw the woman pass with her little suitcases, the supply apparently undiminished.

"Now we are going!" cried the children.

"Shut up!" said the mother.

Another tremendous crash, a great grinding and clatter, and the train began to move.

I should have bought ten of those toy valises, I thought. At least ten. I could have done that for the poor woman. I twisted my neck to see if I could still see her. Yes. There she stood with her basket. I felt that she was looking at me, though we had moved too far away to be sure. She was still standing there as a curve in the track put us out of sight.

I was on my way. Not yet a bona fide missionary, not quite yet. But soon . . .

It was impossible to arrange my knees comfortably in the short space between the seats, for they had been built for Ecuadorians. I had never thought of myself as tall—I was of average height in my own country—until I rode in Ecuadorian buses where I could not stand up straight. A cold draft blew up from the floorboards of the squeaking, creaking train and I tried to twine my legs together to keep them warm. Once a position was found, the effort of changing it was too great, and my lower extremities were soon numb. I decided to ignore this, and turned my attention to the passing scenery.

The track wound through cobblestone streets lined with whitewashed adobe walls and stone-block buildings much like those of Ambato and other sierra towns. I would be glad to leave cities behind now, and reach at last the limitless freedom and purity of the high Andes.

When the train reached the outskirts of the city the dusty dirt roads, lined with mud walls which seemed to have grown out of them, depressed me, as the vast slum areas which circled the city of Guayaquil had depressed me. But somehow, Riobamba's poor did not seem quite so poor, nor its squalor quite so squalid as Guayaquil's. There were garbage heaps in doorways here, there were half-clad, filthy-faced children, some of them boys with shoulder-length hair (for, an Ecuadorian had told me, "If you cut their hair before they learn to talk, they'll never talk"), there were the same rows of windowless houses with tiny shops squeezed into the doorways and strange things floating in great copper basins of boiling oil set on charcoal braziers on the street, there were the blaring radios and, in even less prosperous districts, the empty stillness, as though a plague had carried off all the inhabitants. But as the train crept hesitantly toward the countryside, through the widening streets and more sparsely scattered hovels, I wondered whether I had become so accustomed to poverty that it no longer seemed deplorable to me, or whether it was perhaps the clearness of the mountain air with its blue sky and sunshine and absence of vultures that made Guayaquil's poverty seem, in retrospect, extreme.

For days I had waited in the port city for my baggage to be unloaded from the barges which lay at anchor in the Guayas River. I had nothing at all to do. The days melted into one another, a long, monotonous succession of almost unendurably hot mornings, afternoons and evenings. One day I had seen a man with no eyes and no feet who sat on the pavement with his back against a building, holding a hat to the passersby, his head lolling back on his neck. Two holes where his eyes had been were directed toward me. A girl of about eight lay in his lap, emaciated and limp, with

[6]

immense black eyes rimmed with shadows and shining with fever. She gazed up into my face without a sound. Her lips were dry, her mouth hung slightly open, and flies crawled around the edges of her hair. I stopped, stunned by the sight, and tried to think what to do. The Bible story of Peter and John and the lame man came to mind. The man had asked for money and been healed instead. If only I could give the man his sight, the child her health! I couldn't, so, like Peter and John, I said, "Such as I have give I thee," and dropping a few coins into the greasy hat turned away.

And what of the woman this morning, selling toy suit-cases? I could still see her face, turned toward me as the train had taken me out of sight. I could, of course, have bought the whole lot of toys. Then, I argued with myself, where would she have been? Not very far ahead. And next week? What could I have done to be of any lasting use? Physical help for the man and child in Guayaquil, eco-nomic help for the woman in Riobamba (and for the dozens of beggars I had met in the intervening time)— always the same problem: what to do? Witness to them! came the answer. Missionary reports were always full of such cases, but the aim was supposed to be spiritual work. I found it hard to acknowledge that spiritual need was not somehow correlative to physical, and when confronted with especially pitiful individuals I struggled consciously with the mandate to tell them of Christ. Was it the voice of God, the voice of a dozen preachers I had heard, the voice of an enlightened conscience—or were these voices synon-ymous? In a dusty, high-ceilinged Sunday-school room with worn red carpets and a picture of the Good Shepherd at the front I had learned the Westminster Shorter Cate-chism: "The chief end of man is to glorify God and enjoy Him forever." Then, in a missionary service in another church years later I heard that the chief end of man is to stop as many as possible of the millions from perishing. "Witness to them! Speak to at least one soul a day—remember, they are headed for blackness of darkness"—and here the preacher shook his jowls—"FOREVER!" I was so appalled that I had not stopped to sort out the confusions the two ideas had brought to my mind. I had gone through life with a vague but constant consciousness of having left undone the most vital of things I ought to have done. Others did them, and told about them triumphantly: how they had spoken to a seatmate on a bus, a gasoline station operator, a hairdresser or a ticket agent. Whenever I determined to lay hold of such an opportunity it seemed to evaporate. But when I reached my destination things would be different.

A cinder blew into my eye and I turned from the train window to find my handkerchief.

"She is crying," I heard one of the three children say. I looked to find them all staring enthralled at the *gringa*. How long had they been watching me? I smiled, but again they pretended not to see. Their mother turned then and gazed directly at me, her curiosity undisguised. It was unsettling enough to have a foreigner on the train. It was unbearable that the foreigner should be crying. She saw, however, that I was not crying, and spoke in a whisper to the children, who stopped staring. Soon one of them, a charming five- or six-year-old with a frayed pink ribbon in her luxuriant black curls, came over to where I sat.

"Good morning, señorita," she began. "You are crying, aren't you?"

"Oh no! Something got in my eye. What is your name?"

"Felicita. And yours?"

"Margarita. Are you going to the coast?"

"Why is your hair red?" she asked, paying no attention to my question.

"Red? Do you think my hair is red?"

"Yes. Very red. Why is it red?"

My hair, I thought, was brown—perhaps it had a few reddish lights in it at times, but certainly no one had ever called it red. I had wished it were. Anything but this nondescript brown.

"Your hair is a beautiful black, Felicita. How lucky you are!"

"Why do you wear glasses?"

"Felicita!" Her mother had overheard the question. "Come here."

I smiled at the wide-eyed child. "Go quickly, but come back if your mother says you may."

She went back to her seat, on which she knelt, her chin resting on two small hands placed on the back of the seat. She continued to gaze earnestly at me, pondering the strangeness of this stranger. She *was* crying, and her hair *is* red, and she thinks mine is beautiful and why does she wear those glasses and that ugly coat? (I had on a trenchcoat, belted at the waist, bulky with a sweater underneath.) Why does the *gringa* keep smiling at me? She doesn't know me.

Yes, Felicita, I thought, I am an oddity to you. You would never understand what I am doing here.

There was only honest puzzlement in her face. In a child in Guayaquil I had seen, I thought, resentment. Was it I who had changed? Perhaps I had been overly sensitive to being an alien. There was a woman selling *empanadas*—a kind of turnover—on the sidewalk under an umbrella-covered stand. She had a child hung in a cloth from her shoulder, a long-legged thin boy of at least two who was pulling noisily on her pale breast. She fried the pastries on a tiny stove, turning them with a great perforated ladle, shouting *"Empanadas!"* as she lifted the flaky things from their immersion in the reeking oil and dropped them onto the pile in a washbasin. She took me in at a glance, swiftly comprehending all she wanted to know of me, from head to toe. She had her black hair fastened in a braid with a bit of brown wool entwined in it, and wore a faded cotton dress with the snaps open down the front, a stained apron of heavy duck, black scuffs on her short, wide feet and the look of knowing all on her hard face. The child's hair nearly covered his eyes as he peeked up sideways at me from the source of nourishment. "This is mine," he seemed to be saying to me, "and my mother is mine and we belong here in the center of the whole world, and who are you?"

A displaced person, I had felt—neither at home, nor yet in my appointed niche—but just as I was recalling the uneasiness of that moment I saw from the train a group of Indians trotting by on their way to market in the city, each with a lumpy shawl on his back stuffed with wares to sell. There, I thought to myself, goes my reason for being here. "Go ye into all the world, and preach the Gospel to every creature. . . ." You would never believe it, Felicita, but I belong here. I am under orders.

A low ceiling of mist still lay over the city, and the smoke from the little mud houses spread itself under the mist. Sunlight slanted through in places, exposing an un-made bed through an open doorway here, a cluttered counter in a shop there. Then the railroad track began to rise slightly. For a few seconds we were closed in cloud. Thus blinded I became aware of the sound of the train wheels on the track. They clattered and thumped, thumped and clattered. Suddenly we emerged into sunlight again. There, to the north of us, rose Chimborazo, glittering pure and proud in the morning sun, its tremendous shoulders smooth with snow, the deep ravines blue with shadow against them. The lower slopes, covered with brown grass, spread and spread and spread, out onto the misty *páramo*, patches of brown in varying shades showing where Indians had cultivated. The motion and the noise of the train faded again from my awareness and the city receded behind us. The maguey-lined roads we were passing, with eucalyptus groves and tile-roofed shacks, were blurred. I saw only the peak, that clear peak, radiant, towering, full of strength and peace. It drew me as it had never drawn me in the months when I saw it from Ambato. I felt magnetized, yet its cold brilliance and total inaccessibility cowed me at the same time that it drew me. The winding of the railroad track took me out of range again and once more I smelled the damp wool in front of me, the banana peels on the floor, the smoke of the engine.

"Here I am," I thought, with a muffled kind of excitement, wanting to savor every part. God knew the whole picture when He called me here, but I would have to find it out little by little. He knew the beginning and the ending and everything that fitted in between. For me, the beginning had been six years before. I was nineteen then, and had just finished my sophomore year in Bible college. A missionary from Africa was to speak and show slides at church. It was a very warm night, and a week night too, not a Sunday. Going to church would necessitate washing my hair and ironing a dress and it was too hot to do either, but the man was a friend of the family, my father was a pillar of the church and a great supporter of missions, and it was unthinkable for the Sparhawks not to attend, en masse, such a meeting.

He spoke on a verse from the Bible, "I the Lord have called thee." He emphasized the word "thee." I had heard a hundred missionaries speak, I had looked at thousands of slides, of which a large percentage showed natives of one color or another lined up with smiles on their faces before thatched church buildings. There was nothing distinctive about either the man or the message on that July evening, but there was something peculiarly personal—I could neither explain nor ignore it—about the way those words sounded to me then. "I the Lord have called *thee.*"

Not that the idea of being a missionary was new to me. Not by any means. I had talked about the possibility since I was a small child. My aunt was a missionary in India and she sent me little brass bells and brought me a cobra-skin purse when she came home on furlough. She always stayed at our house for several months out of a year's furlough, and we had a picture of her in an elaborate brass frame—she was dressed in a sari and had a little brown baby in her arms—on the living-room table. I think my father, who almost worshipped her, secretly hoped that I would feel called to join her in the orphanage work. He was a construction engineer who tithed his income very carefully. He had wanted to be a missionary, he said, or at least go into what he called "full-time Christian work," but the Lord had showed him that He could use businessmen too, and He wanted my father to support missionaries rather than to be one. So he taught a Sunday-school class, belonged to a group of businessmen dedicated to winning their colleagues to Christ, and brought his children up in the fear of the Lord. One of my brothers had gone into the construction business on his own, and the other was in seminary preparing to be a minister. My father could not take issue with either choice, but he still hoped most fervidly that one of his children would go to the foreign field for the Lord. My little sister, four years younger than I, was the darling of the family, and although she talked about being a missionary nurse I felt that my parents were not really eager to see her leave her native shores.

Once, when I was about eleven, a visiting preacher had thundered about the unwillingness of Christians to "sell out" for God. We sang for the closing hymn "Is your all on the altar?" and he moved from the pulpit down to the altar rail and asked those of us who "really meant business" to come forward.

> You cannot have rest, and be perfectly blest,
> Until all on the altar is laid,

sang the congregation. I knew that I wanted to be blessed, I meant business with God, so whatever it was that needed to be laid on the altar I was determined to lay. I went forward.

There had been other times, too. In missionary meetings when volunteers were called for, I had never been sure enough to stand up, but usually an invitation was given for those who would be willing to go if the Lord should call. I stood up for that one. Now, it seemed to me, He had called. But the missionary from Africa did not ask anyone to stand or come forward. He did not even ask for a show of hands. For a moment I felt cheated, but then I was glad, for when I went home and knelt down alone in my room to pray I was confident that I had not been merely the victim of an emotional appeal, a public altar demonstration, but that I had indeed heard the call of the Lord, commissioning me to be His ambassador in some far-off place. India, perhaps, but that was not important to me just then. "Lord," I prayed, "I think You meant me tonight, and if I am not mistaken that it is You that have called, give me one more sign—tomorrow morning—to confirm it."

Next morning when I went to breakfast there was a copy of *Mary Slessor of Calabar* at my place. I found an inscription in the flyleaf: "To Margaret, with the prayer that this great missionary's life may inspire you, and that the Lord may lead you to the place of His choice. Love, Mother." How had she known? I had said nothing to her or anyone else. Clearly, this was the sign I had prayed for. I ate my toast and drank my coffee with a sense of wonder at the destiny that had been shown me. Only my sister was at the table—the others had eaten earlier—but I said nothing to her.

I went into the living room afterward and stood looking at the carved wood motto which hung over the mantelpiece: "Fear thou not, for I am with thee." This, too, was the voice of God. The motto had hung there for as long as I could remember—sometimes partly hidden by a vase of flowers or by Christmas cards or family pictures or missionary curios which were later relegated to the attic—and I had looked at it without seeing it, but today it spoke to me, and the words "thou" and "thee" were in italics.

Now the train was passing through a desert area. Tall cactus, thick with dust, lined the railroad track. Sand was banked along the road which ran beside us and the wind blew it through the cracks of the windows and along the floor of the carriage. The sun was high now, shining on the dry landscape, and it seemed that it ought to be hot, but the cold wind kept wrapping around my legs. The snowcap was hidden from view by a hill now. A woman hurried alone up a stony path, her shawl pulled tightly across her mouth, her head pushing into the wind. No other human being was in sight.

I began to feel sleepy, and tried to lean my head against the window. The vibration was too much and my head dropped and snapped miserably, but I could not hold it erect. I slept a little and dreamed I was riding a subway on a snowy night, returning to Bible school with fellow students.

There was the sudden woof-woof of a whistle. The brakes screamed. Had we reached a station? I lifted my head. A flock of sheep was tumbling across the tracks, followed by a frantic woman waving a stick. Spread out on all sides was a valley, green and brown and gray, dotted with hundreds of grass-roofed huts, scored with earthen walls and maguey-plant fences, rows of dark-green, stiff-pointed clusters. The mountains swept up on both sides in vast, easy slopes as though some huge hand had smoothed them back from the floor of the valley, in which lay a great sheet of water, feathered with reeds and flecked with white birds. A field of tall wheat breathed in the wind, gently rising and sinking like a living thing in the sunlight. The sky was wide and brilliant blue, an immense canopy flung from the points of the mountains over this paradise beneath. The size of the valley made the speed of the train seem to diminish almost to a crawl. As we rounded the shore of the lake I could see Indians sitting astride their rush rafts in the water. They were gathering something in the reeds—perhaps it was the reeds themselves. No doubt that was it, I thought, for I had seen the mats they sold in the markets of Ambato, and had heard they were made from lake grass.

[15]

The little mud houses were everywhere. Nowhere in Ecuador had I seen so many. They seemed to peep suspiciously at me from under the shaggy, steeply-pitched roofs, like the child who had peeped at me so smugly from his mother's breast.

"Look on the fields, for they are white already unto harvest. . . . Pray ye therefore the Lord of the harvest, that He would send forth labourers into his harvest. . . ."

I had come. Here were the fields, teeming and ready.

"AND DID you find the train trip hard, dear?" Mrs. Mac-Donald passed me a cup of tea.

"Oh no," I said, "I was a little sleepy since I had to get up very early, but the scenery was so beautiful I didn't think much about the train itself."

"Not what you're used to in the United States, is it, though? I hear they've beautiful trains there." Mrs. Mac-Donald's t's and r's were still Scottish, though she said she had been away from her homeland for many years. She poured a cup of tea, moved an empty cup closer, and poured the tea from the first cup into the second. I watched with interest.

"And now you're wondering what it is I'm doing," she said, her pink cheeks lifting in a smile. "Oh, it's a funny custom. Ian likes his cup warmed first, so I pour him another one. That way he gets it really hot." She moved the sugar bowl toward me.

"Ian. Ian, dearie?" she called.

"I'm coming, Janet. Coming right away." He came into the room through a doorway covered by a flowered curtain. His feet scraped slightly as he moved. He paused a moment and looked steadily at us both—first at his wife, then at me. His hands trembled almost imperceptibly as he put them on the back of his chair and pulled it slowly out from the table. He smiled and sat down.

"Some of your oat cakes, dearie. I thought maybe Margaret would like them too. My mother used to make these," she said, lifting the china plate of little brown biscuits and passing it to me. "Ian likes them very much. But I can't get quite the right kind of oats here. I have to substitute."

"They never tasted better to me in Scotland," said Ian, picking one up almost tenderly. He lifted his face and closed his eyes. "Father," he said, "You've given us all things good, and we thank You from our hearts. Amen."

I had heard many prayers in my life, but few with which I so wholeheartedly joined. It was exactly what I wanted to say. The marvel of that broad valley with its lake and white birds and straw huts and mountain bastions; then the trip through the pass and up into further hills, across more desert and through fields of calla lilies, lovely in their classic simplicity, then the arrival at the Wairapamba railroad station, where I saw the kind face (like the Good Shepherd, I had thought at once) of Mr. MacDonald looking over the shoulders of some Indians who were waiting; now this room, with its sunlight coming through the geraniums on the windowsill, the taste of the hot tea and the crumbly cakes—for all of this, and for the honest warmth of the two people who had received me, I was more grateful than an elaborate prayer could have expressed. "All things good. We thank You."

It was as I had hoped. If God had called me to Ecuador there would be a sense of belonging, a confidence that things were as they should be. During those strange and uneasy first days in the country this confidence had been lacking, and I had wondered whether I had made a mistake.

The certainty of my call seemed to wane, perhaps at times because of the oppressive heat, perhaps because of the shock of finding myself an alien. My mind was soon at rest when such explanations could be found. When they could not, I was troubled. Why was it, for example, when I helped a group of missionaries in Guayaquil with the task of folding Gospel tracts, that their conversation seemed somehow staged? They spoke of people in terms of "souls," cities in terms of "need," and church meetings in terms of attendance. Not that I would at that time have found fault with this view. Far from it. The fault lay, I suspected, with myself in not being able wholeheartedly to share it. Had I not been called to cast in my lot with these servants of the Lord?

But here in the MacDonald home things were different. I found a peace and a simplicity, which acted like a balm to my spirit. The teacups were of bone china, and the spoons were thin sterling—they must be very old, I thought, probably an heirloom from Mrs. MacDonald's family. The furniture was crude and heavy, of Ecuadorian design. They lived neither in unrelieved ugliness nor in inappropriate luxury, it seemed to me, and I was reminded of home, where a few very beautiful things that had been given to us, such as an Oriental rug and a cloisonné vase, were mingled with practical and inexpensive things which my parents, who considered all their money the Lord's, had bought.

"You can't imagine how we've prayed for this," Mr. MacDonald said to me. "You know we thought we were going to work with the Indians. Thirty-one years ago we came to these mountains, selling Bibles in the little villages round about. We couldn't sell many—not many people could read, and they were afraid of us. They would see us coming. Foreigners. And they'd run. But God gave us some precious opportunities. There's an old brother who lives seven miles from here who bought one of those first Bibles. He couldn't read, but he'd always wanted a book. 'If I had a book, I could learn to read,' he had said. 'If only I had a book.' So when I came he said, 'That's what I want. I want that book.' His wife scolded him for wasting money. He didn't give her any heed. He went into the back room and I could hear him moving trunks and things. He must have kept his money in one of them. His wife was screaming at him, 'So you'll let the children starve, you won't buy me a good rooster, but you'll buy a book.' Well, he bought it, and he learned to read. I came back several years later and he was reading. He knows the book now, from cover to cover. And I think he knows the Author, too. So you see, Margaret lassie, the Lord knows what He's about." He passed the cakes to me again, and his cup to Mrs. MacDonald. She poured milk into it and then tea.

"But you were telling Margaret about our wanting to do Indian work, dearie. You do get off the track."

"Oh yes. We came here to live twenty-eight years ago. We had sold Bibles in the area for a few years—I think it was five years—and then we came here to live. We visited around with the people of the town and with the Indians in the hills. But the Indians only come to town on market day and they live far apart. We found we couldn't keep them here long enough to do any work with them, and we couldn't visit their homes often enough. We had the children, you know." He took a sip of tea.

"How many do you have?" I asked.

"We have three," Mrs. MacDonald answered, her eyes lighting. "Two lassies and a laddie."

"Isn't your son a missionary?" I asked.

"Oh yes—in Tanganyika. He's been there two years now and just last week we received a letter from him with the news that he's found a wife. She's an English girl—a nurse. They won't be married for another year or so—she's still studying the language. But we're so happy for him. You know, it doesn't seem right for a young man to be alone like that, away out there." She had risen from her chair with the teapot in her hands. She looked eagerly at me. "I'll show you the picture he sent of her. She looks like a dear girl. And here I am talking when your cup is empty. I'll just heat this up a wee bit." She went to the kerosene stove in the corner of the room, set the teapot on the side and poured water from the steaming kettle into it. Her husband watched her bent back from the other side of the room. She straightened up and stretched a wisp of white hair into the cluster of pins at the back of her head, looked at the clock, and then carried the teapot to the table again.

"Here, Margaret dear, let me fill your cup. You must be tired. No? Ah, you're young. And then we have the two girls—Joan is married to a doctor in Kansas and Mary's studying to be a teacher. Sometimes we wonder about Mary." She looked at the geraniums with her head angled slightly to one side. She lifted her cup and held it without drinking. "Ah, she's a dear girlie. She had a hard time being away from us at the first, and then later, somehow she didn't seem to want to come back home. She didn't write for five weeks once. We heard things from people in Scotland: Mary's running around, Mary's not going to church, Mary's a wee bit rebellious. We don't know. The Lord knows what she needs, and we just commit her to Him. He's the Shepherd of the sheep—He won't let His lambs go astray. That we know, don't we, Ian? But we've talked too much, and you must want a little nap, Margaret.

[21]

We haven't heard anything about you, dear, and we want to—tomorrow you'll tell us all about yourself—but not now. You're tired. Come. Let me show you your room. Ah, you don't know how good it is to have you with us. We prayed so long that the Lord would send someone who could work with our Indians." She put her hands on the edge of the table and pushed herself back and then up from the chair. "You'll love them. I know you'll love them. But you won't find it easy."

"No, I don't expect I will. Everyone tells me how hard they are to reach. But then nothing's too hard for the Lord." As soon as the words were out of my mouth I felt checked. Who was I to tell a veteran missionary such a thing? Mrs. MacDonald put her arm around my waist.

"Follow the Shepherd, Margaret. He knows the way. I will fear no evil, for Thou art with me. That's His promise —to be with us. Ian and I have known it here."

The room to which she showed me was very small and immaculately clean, with a chair, a dresser and a bed that had a crocheted spread on it.

"There now, dear, you just put your things here." She pulled back a curtain and showed me a closet. "And there in the dresser is drawer space. You'll need a wee nap, now. You just lie down there, and when supper is ready I'll call you."

She left me and I went to the window, which looked out on a small patio where there were a dovecote and a great many geraniums in brilliant bloom. I saw Mrs. MacDonald open the kitchen door. The doves burbled and cooed as she held up her hands to them.

"*Palomita, palomita!*" she called, as though they would understand her better in Spanish than in English, and obediently they flew to her, circled and picked up the crumbs she scattered.

On the dresser was a neat, fat pincushion, crocheted like the bedspread, and a crystal bud vase with a few corn-flowers. There was a plaster-of-Paris motto on the wall with the words "He careth for you" entwined with forget-me-nots and rosebuds.

I could have wished that the little room, in the quiet home, in the town of Wairapamba, were for me the end of the road. It might have been so, for the mission to which I belonged, Indians for Christ, Incorporated, had suggested that I settle there near the MacDonalds, at least until the arrival of the Gardners, a couple who were coming to work with me but had so far been delayed for medical reasons. But Wairapamba was not so centrally located for reaching the Quichuas as some of the smaller towns farther up in the mountains, and the mission, as well as the Mac-Donalds, was pleased to know that I was willing to start out alone in the attempt to gain a footing among the people whom I thought of as my own. Tomorrow the Mac-Donalds were to drive me in their jeep up to Indi Urcu, several hours away, and help me to move into the house they had procured for me.

I lay down on the bed and thought about all the way which the Lord had led me. There was a certain element of apprehension of the unknown as I contemplated my arrival in Indi Urcu, but the knowledge that the MacDonalds had prayed for someone to work with the Indians, when they had found that they themselves could not, was to me the final seal that the course I had chosen was God's course.

There had been some strained moments at home when my parents learned that not only was I not going to India

[23]

with my aunt, but that I intended to apply to a small, newly organized mission instead of to an established one, and would probably end up in Ecuador. Ecuador! They were not even sure where it was, and they had never known anyone who had gone there. Africa, China, India— these were the known fields. Why Ecuador? I had finally succeeded in persuading them that it was God's will. The evidence was enough for me—a chance encounter with a missionary, a meeting in which the needs of Ecuador's Indians were presented, a series of circumstances which seemed to point toward my going there, and, most incontestable of all, an inner conviction that this was it. I did not try to prove it to others. I simply said that the Lord was leading me, and this was both understandable and believable to my family and friends. I had not thought much about how such a statement might appear to others until I happened to meet a young man in Guayaquil, a drug salesman from New Jersey named Bill who, when he learned that I was a missionary, said, "A missionary! God. What's your religion?"

The question took me off guard. I belonged to a small church called interdenominational where we thought of all religions as sadly mistaken. Ours, by contrast, was not called a religion at all. It was the Way. Believing this as I did, the only answer I could think of sounded lame.

"Well, I'm a Protestant. I'm hoping to work among Indians and translate the Bible for them."

"Going to work in the jungle, huh?"

"No—among mountain Indians. Quichuas."

"Mountain Indians! Jesus Christ. Do you think you'll like that?"

"Oh, I think so."

"Kinda tough for a girl. Some of those mountain Indians

[24]

can be pretty tough." He shook his head slowly and surveyed me as though assessing my capabilities for the job. "Well, I wish you luck. I suppose you've got the call, haven't you?"

"Yes," I said, wondering how I could change the subject, for it was not clear what "the call" might mean to Bill, and I cringed at the thought of trying to explain to him what it meant to me. "Do you like your work?"

"Oh yeah, it's a good job. Good pay, lots of travel, meet a lot of nice people. It's only a job, though—the work is all cut out, you put in your time, draw your salary. But take you—you've got something to do that's really worthwhile —if you can *get* anywhere with those Indians."

There was nothing to say to this. I smiled. It was true, I thought, that what I had to do was far more than a job, and there was no salary. My support had been partially pledged by individuals who wanted to have a part in missionary work. There was no guarantee, of course, that they would fulfill these pledges, and even if they did the amount would not cover my expenses. I was living on faith, which I had been taught was a very honorable position of dependence on the Lord, never to be confused with living on charity, which meant dependence on human beings. As for having my work cut out, as Bill had, there were moments when I wished that the term "missionary" were a little more clearly definable. If I had been a missionary teacher or doctor or nurse my goals would have seemed unequivocal. Just how I was to "get anywhere" with the Indians I was not sure.

"I knew a couple of missionaries in Colombia once," Bill went on. "I was up there before I came here. Couple of girls. Nice girls, they were, from New York. They invited me down to their apartment one night for dinner. I was glad—you know, a bachelor, living alone, eating out in restaurants a lot, traveling a lot—it had been a long time since I had a good old American home-cooked meal. So I was glad they asked me. I tried to think of something I could take to those girls. You know what I mean, some little thing. So I bought a bottle of Drambuie. There's just nothing like a little glass of Drambuie with your after-dinner coffee. I thought it was just the thing. So I arrived at their house and when they opened the door I could smell steaks broiling. I gave them this bottle—and you know what they did? *They threw me out*. They took one look at the bottle and they threw me out. Really. I couldn't believe it. Never even gave me the meal they'd cooked. Can you beat that?"

"Oh, I suppose some missionaries are like that. It *is* hard to believe, though. I hope we're not all alike."

There was a low murmur from the kitchen, where Mr. and Mrs. MacDonald were. They did not want to wake me, and I could hear her moving plates and pans and things very gently as she prepared supper. Now and then a white dove flashed across the square of sky that I could see as I lay on the bed. It was delicious not to sleep, but just to lie in the stillness and think.

"Thank God," I thought, "they are not all alike."

CHAPTER

IT TOOK a long time to get ready for the trip to Indi Urcu the next morning. Mrs. MacDonald packed a lunch of sandwiches, oat cakes and several thermos bottles of tea. She had to feed the doves and chickens and close all the shutters in the house against robbery, for which mountain Indians were famous. Mr. MacDonald went to the gas station and filled two jeep cans with gasoline because there would be none available farther up in the hills. It took me no time to assemble my few things and then I offered to help Mrs. MacDonald, but she said, "Oh, thank you, dear, no dear, I'll just put these plants away from the window and then we'll be ready." She scurried about, finding things to do, glancing now and again at the clock, making sure the doors were locked, and then she took off her apron, tucked in a strand of hair, put on a coat and said, "Now. Is Ian ready? Ian's all ready, I think. We can go now, dear. Do you have a coat? Good girlie. It does get cold up in the mountains." Her husband was just loading some boards into the back of the jeep. They might be needed for bridging an irrigation channel or a washed-out place in the road, he explained.

The trip was long and very bumpy and dusty, but I did

not mind it at all. It was a comfortable feeling to be sitting between two veteran servants of the Lord, people who knew the country and the Indians, who were profoundly concerned with the work I had come to do, people I could trust. Other journeys in Ecuador had been alone: the endless trip by bus, ferry and train to Ambato when I could not speak Spanish and kept waking up all night long, fearful lest I should sleep through the stop where I was supposed to get off, or waken to find my purse gone; the bouncing ride from Ambato to Riobamba when I was squeezed against the window by an enormous man dressed in black with a gold-headed cane who kept smiling and leaning toward me, breathing garlic and asking in English, "What ees your name? Where are you going?"

For the first few miles out of Wairapamba the people whom we passed waved in recognition of the jeep and the MacDonalds. "Oh, now there goes a dear lady, Margaret. My, what a story! Her husband drowned himself and left her with five children and shortly after that twelve sheep that she was keeping for someone else were struck by lightning, and then her youngest child died of smallpox. She accepted a New Testament one day when we visited her and now she's just a radiant Christian, such a dear soul. Oh my, Margaret, if you could know her!" A man rode by on horseback and waved to us. He was a *simpatizante*, they said, very friendly and open to the Gospel. A priest in a brown robe and sandals raised his hand and nodded—the MacDonalds had had some long talks with him. "There are many true believers in the Church, I think, Margaret," Mr. MacDonald said. "Oh, I think we're going to be surprised to see who's there when we get to heaven. 'He that is not against us is for us,' Jesus said. He alone knows who they are. And then there are those we expect to see who won't be there—Not every one who says 'Lord, Lord' will enter the Kingdom of Heaven. Ah, it sobers me to think of it."

The rest of the journey was like the day before—great stretches of brown grass, patchwork of cultivated fields, maguey borders, Indians trotting in both directions, scarcely looking at the car, then turning their faces away to avoid the dust; sheep and cattle and horses, a few goats, even a pair of llamas looking over a broken mud wall near a thatched house. And on all sides the mountains rising toward the burning blue sky, with the snow-covered cone of Chimborazo always in view. We stopped beside a small stream to eat our lunch. The grass grew lushly green beside it, but before we got out of the car Mrs. MacDonald whispered to me to be careful walking in the grass. "You know the habits of the Indians, dear. One has to be careful." It was well that she had warned me, for although I had learned to watch my step near towns and villages, the freshness of the mountain air and the glorious cleanness of the wide landscape might have given me a false confidence. Mr. MacDonald spread a blanket for us and his wife unpacked the sandwiches and laid them in neat piles and then poured tea. It was quiet except for the far-off bleat of a sheep. Occasional cloud shadows floated over us but we were protected from the wind in the shallow ravine where the brook ran.

We drove on after lunch, the road becoming increasingly rutted and winding so that I marveled to find that the jeep kept going. No one seemed inclined to talk, and I sat with my thoughts. Here, now is the land of my adoption. I had heard missionaries use the term affectionately. "Yes, dear friends, my heart is in Africa, land of my adoption, and I long to return." Upon my arrival in Guayaquil I had tried to arrange the furniture of my mind to include the dim light bulbs in the hotel, the short sheets on the bed, the lukewarm water from the tap which I dared not drink without boiling, the towels that looked like dresser scarves. These things had not satisfied my idea of missionary hardship and I knew that I would have to wait until I got into my real work.

When I had walked the streets of the port city, my heart sick at the sight of the beggars with their streaming eyes and the precarious bamboo houses leaning against modern steel and concrete structures, I had felt almost offended that such poverty should exist. I had looked at the emaciated children in the slums and the empty faces along the waterfront and had thought of Jesus, weeping over a great city, for they were as sheep without a shepherd. What sacrifice would I not make, I had asked myself, to meet such need? Why is it that no one does anything about it *now?* As soon as I learn Spanish . . . But, of course, I was not called to those people. It was to the Indians of the highlands that I had been called, and now, as the village where I would live came into view around the shoulder of a hill, I wanted to give notice that help was on the way. A woman carrying an enormous clay water jar passed us, and I wondered if she might someday be a friend of mine who, when she saw me, would call out, *"Buenos días,* Señorita Margarita!" and be glad that I had come to the mountains. The street we entered first was cobblestone and perfectly empty, with rows of squat, whitewashed houses on both sides, windows shuttered and doors closed. A door opened, an arc of dirty water splashed into the street, and the door banged shut. Someday, perhaps, that door would open to let me in.

"This is Indi Urcu, Margaret," said Mr. MacDonald, "Hill of the Sun." The sun shone down on the dusty cobblestones, and little eddies of wind drew circles in the corners of the doorways. Each corner we passed revealed identical streets, empty and silent. Then a man driving an ancient donkey loaded with round metal water tanks went by, switching the beast with eucalyptus twigs. The flanks of the donkey were great sculptures of bone, swathed in mouse-colored skin so thin that it looked as though it might at any moment give way. The animal moved without modifying in the slightest his creaking pace, the switch falling regularly on his back, the two heavy cans scraping his sides. Someday, I hoped, the love of God would get through to that man, and he would learn to love his burro.

When we reached the plaza in the center of the little town the car was instantly stormed by energetic women with baskets.

"Choclos! Choclos a un sucre! Queso!" They bleated at us, thrusting their wares through the windows. Mr. MacDonald smiled and nudged his way gently through the little knot of people. Market was over for the day, so the rest of the plaza was nearly empty. A few people came to the doorways of small shops to watch the *gringos* pass, and an Indian woman who had just knelt on the steps of the Catholic church turned her head to gaze after us, still kneeling. Would she, too, perhaps someday know the liberty of the Gospel of Jesus Christ? Was she, like most of the Indians, Catholic in name only, and lacking in any personal relationship with Christ? How much of her native ignorance and superstition were bound up in the only form of worship she knew? I wanted to guide her far beyond forms and ceremonies to the living Savior.

Mr. MacDonald drove up another side street and stopped at a doorway where a woman with an apron and dangling earrings gave him the key to my house. We could see that she wanted him to come in, but with a gracious bowing and gesturing in the Latin way he explained that we could not take the time. The lady nodded to us and we drove away, up the hill to a street where grass grew between the cobblestones and each house had a tiny yard enclosed by white adobe walls.

"Here we are, Margaret dear. This one is your little house. Oh, and the geraniums I planted are blooming so nicely!" Mrs. MacDonald patted my hand. The house was low, with a rust-colored tile roof and small-paned windows with shutters.

"Oh, Ian dear, you must fix the latches on those shutters! I thought we'd shut them when we left last time!" said Mrs. MacDonald in dismay. The whitewash on the adobe walls was dusty and the door was unpainted. I liked these touches. They made it seem a quaint and rustic cottage. I will be happy here, I thought.

While Mr. MacDonald unlocked the door I turned to look at the view from the front gate. The main part of the town lay below us, and I could see over the roofs and far across the valley, where hundreds of thatched houses—Indian houses, I thought joyfully—studded the plain like haymows. I saw that the MacDonalds had chosen the location wisely, and my eye drew imaginary lines, like the spokes of a wheel, from the gateway to the little houses—that one with the smoke filtering through the roof, the one over there on that knoll, that tiny one I could barely see in the haze of the distance. Unreached, every one of them, but, God helping me, I would reach them.

"Come in, dear." Mrs. MacDonald beckoned me inside, and I surveyed my home, the first I could call my own. There were only a few things in it—a small table, a chair, a chamber pot in the bedroom and a set of rusty springs, besides the bigger pieces of my baggage and furniture which Mr. MacDonald had brought up a couple of days before. We unloaded the things from the jeep, including a box of food which Mrs. MacDonald had prepared for me, enough to last for several days. She went about from room to room, mentally placing me in each one, anxiously arranging the things she knew I had brought and questioning me about other things she was sure I would need. Eager to show her that I could manage, I went into the kitchen and made tea and we sat on boxes and foot lockers in the living room while we drank it.

"You'll be all right here now, won't you, dear?" she said. I thanked her for all they had done—finding the house, cleaning it, transporting my things, bringing me. They were to spend the night in a room at the landlady's house since there was no hotel and there were not beds enough in my house for three.

"We'll just pop round in the morning, then, dear, to see that you're all right," she said. "Oh my, how we thank God that you've come, Margaret! How we prayed, didn't we, Ian? And now you've come!" She gave my shoulders a squeeze, her husband tipped his hat to me, opened the door and gently helped her into the jeep. I watched them move slowly down the street, Mrs. MacDonald's handkerchief fluttering from the window.

THE HOUSE seemed very empty indeed, and I felt more alone than ever before. It was not loneliness, exactly. Nor was it the feeling of alienation I had known since I arrived in the country. It was, rather, the aloneness of responsibility that pressed on me like a weight. Ever since that hot night when I was nineteen I had known that the responsibility lay upon me—I was one of those to whom God had specifically said, "Go *ye*." And now the emptiness, the silence and the damp chill of the thick-walled little house assumed almost a physical presence which confronted me and said, "You. It is you, now, who must act. If you do nothing, nothing will be done."

I went to the window of the living room, where no curtains had yet been hung, and looked across the rooftops of the town to the valley filled with houses. This was the beginning in earnest, and I found in my heart, along with the burden of responsibility, a genuine gratitude to God for the privilege which I saw was mine. He had provided all I needed; He would lead me ("Fear thou not, for I am with thee"—the Scriptural words came as confirmation of my own thought); He was responsible, in the end, for the results.

I looked around the bleak little room. No point in trying to bring order out of chaos tonight. Tomorrow I would arrange things. I pulled some food out of Mrs. MacDonald's box and found enough utensils to fix myself some supper. I could hear the wind whipping around the corners of the house, but there was no other sound. The single light bulb which illuminated the supper table was almost as dim as candlelight. If my friends could see me now! "Oh yes—Margaret Sparhawk. She went to Ecuador, you know —lives all alone way up in the mountains someplace with the Indians. A million Indians, I think she said, up in the Andes." That's what they would say, of course, and I would make light of the hardships, tell them how beautiful it was, how I loved the work, how fascinating the Indians were, really, when you got to know them. . . . But I must write to my friends right away. Another prayer letter was long overdue. I had written my first one from Ambato, but had delayed the second, thinking it would be more interesting to wait until I reached my own station. That was what my friends were eager to hear about.

Rummaging in a file box I found the first circular letter —we had called them "prayer letters" at home, where my parents received every week a dozen or so mimeographed reports from missionaries scattered over the globe. My father would read excerpts aloud at family devotions and we would pray for the writers, mentioning the specific needs stated in the letters. It was virtually the only way missionaries had to keep from being forgotten in prayer and—though this was seldom referred to except obliquely —from being financially neglected. I accepted this method without question as one of God's ways of supplying my needs.

I read over the letter I had written from Ambato.

[35]

Dear praying friends:

When He putteth forth His sheep, He goeth before. The Lord has fulfilled His word to me, and at last I find myself in Ecuador, the country to which He called me three years ago. How thankful I am for the privilege of being an ambassador for Christ! And how grateful I am to you dear ones whose prayers and gifts made it possible for me to obey the Great Commission!

Here I am in Ambato, a beautiful city in the inter-Andean plane, about 7,000 feet above sea level. There are Spanish colonial buildings, burros and pushcarts and modern cars in the streets, palm trees in gardens and patios. I live with a very nice family, Señor Honorio Torres and his friendly, attractive wife, Señora Aïda. He speaks a little English, but she does not know a word, which is an advantage for me because I am forced to speak Spanish. She chatters away very amiably, apparently thinking that I can follow what she says even though I seldom can think how to answer her! The house is very clean and comfortable, and I have a nice little room overlooking the street. Just now as I write I can see a small boy with a huge flat basket of rolls on his head, a shawled woman carrying two live chickens by their legs, a policeman in a khaki uniform with a gleaming white belt who keeps issuing diffident little peeps on a tiny whistle. I wonder why he does this? It seems that if anyone were breaking the law the whistle would give him plenty of warning of the policeman's approach. Well, there are many things in a foreign country that one doesn't understand, but it is interesting to learn, and I have learned to say, "How do you say?" and "What is this?" and "Why?"

Every morning I have a Spanish lesson with a charming young señorita named Dolores who wears very high-heeled shoes, long fancy earrings and such well-cut clothes that I feel at times quite frumpy and timid in her presence. She lives in a huge colonial house with a carved front door and a patio in the center, where a fat Indian woman rubs clothes

[36]

on a block of stone. I have my lesson in an upstairs room which is very dark since it has only one long narrow window. There are immense portraits of bearded gentlemen and solemn ladies—descendants, I suppose, of the *conquistadores* themselves—on the walls, and they are hung diagonally across the four corners of the room and slanted so that their gaze seems to rest on me as I sit at my lesson. My "desk" is a velvet-covered round table, and my teacher sits opposite me on a brocade throne.

"*Rápido, rápido, rápido!*" she shrills at me, snapping her fingers in rhythm with the words, and I struggle to conjugate a verb without faltering, "*Yo hago, tu haces, él hace.*" It is not easy to get them all straight, and I am having an especially difficult time learning the subjunctive, and trying to imitate the intonation pattern, which Señorita Dolores says is very important. My high school Spanish did not get me very far, I am afraid! So please pray for progress in the language study, so that I may soon move out to the Indian villages where I will begin the work to which God has specifically called me.

Pray, too, that I may be a faithful witness for Christ here in this home, and in the city. I am not sure whether the Torres family are true believers, though they are quite willing to discuss the Bible and my reasons for being here in Ecuador. I had a thrilling experience the other day, however, and I trust you will pray very especially for the Lord's blessing in this matter. I went on a picnic with the Torres family—by bus, over the hills to a lovely swimming place in a green valley— and there I got into conversation with a thin, dark-haired girl named Gladys who said that she had some reservations about the Catholic faith and many questions she wanted to ask me about my own. When I said I would love to come to her house (she lived not far from me in Ambato) and read the Bible with her she jumped at the chance. Consequently I have been visiting her almost every day since, and it seems clear that the Lord is working in her heart. I believe He led me to the encounter, and has been directing me in our talks together.

Pray that He will bring her to a definite decision. Perhaps He will give me this seal of approval on my coming, even before I reach the people of the mountains!

I have had correspondence with the MacDonalds, senior missionaries who work up in the mountains, and they have located a good spot for me to work in a Quichua area. I can hardly wait until my time here is up and I can reach at last that needy place. Pray that they may be able to find a suitable house for me when the time comes. Remember to pray, too, for the Gardners, that they may soon receive medical clearance and join me in the work.

Yours in Christ,
Margaret Sparhawk.

Five months had passed now, and it was time to write another letter. How to begin? "Dear praying friends" was a standard beginning, and had seemed all right in Ambato. Something had happened since then, something which seemed to call for a simpler form of address—was it a cooler, calmer view of things which I now took? I was not certain, and although "Dear friends" sounded a trifle dis-tant I could think of no better beginning.

The time spent in Ambato has come to a close, and I want to thank each one of you for your prayers. The study of Spanish was very profitable and my teacher was pleased with my examinations. . . .

Here I am, at last, in Indi Urcu (the *i*'s are pronounced like *e*'s, the *u*'s are long), a little village much higher up in the Andes than Ambato was, in the center of a large Indian area. I am hoping to start the study of Quichua as soon as I can find an informant, and would ask you to pray that the Lord will guide me to the right one. As you know, my ultimate goal is the translation of the Bible into mountain Quichua.

Some of you, perhaps, are wondering about Gladys.

Here I paused, not knowing what to write about a thing which had caused me no end of anxiety and self-criticism. Things had worked beautifully in the beginning, I believed God had led me to her, she seemed as needy as any jungle savage, she was open to all I had to say. I had prayed, friends had prayed, but one week the maid said she was not at home and the next week she said she was sick. The following week she was at home, but told me she did not really want to read the Bible and was having difficulty finding time to study the English verb lists I had given her. In the end, she did not see me any more, and I wondered if after all I was never to qualify as a missionary. What could I tell those who had prayed?

She never came to any definite commitment of herself to Christ, so far as I know, although I believe that the Lord is able to bring fruit out of seed that has been planted. Keep on praying for her.

I paused again. Here, in Indi Urcu, things were bound to happen. Perhaps God was only testing my faith in the Gladys experience. After all, someone has to plant. Often another reaps.

Remember the words of Scripture, "When we believe not, yet He abideth faithful."
Yours for the salvation of Ecuador's Indians,
Margaret Sparhawk.

I rolled the paper out of the machine and started to read it over but realized that my feet were cold. The little house was drafty and the thick adobe walls held the cold. I got up and went to the bedroom to see if I could find my slippers in the jumble of boxes. A window was open and I discovered that the latch did not fit, so I wedged a piece of paper under it. Dust had blown over everything and felt gritty to my fingers as I opened the suitcases. Oh dear, I thought, where am I to hang all these things? There wasn't a closet in the house. But how petty! I scolded myself. Other missionaries had trekked over mountains, across deserts, through raging seas.

> They met the tyrant's brandished steel,
> The lion's gory mane,
> They bowed their necks the death to feel—
> Who follows in their train?

If I were to answer with my own name I had better stop worrying about cold feet, broken latches, dust and lack of closet space.

I DREAMED that I stood on a platform before a vast audience. There was a hush as I opened my mouth to speak. No sound came, and in that endless second of my dream I remembered other dreams in which I had been frightened and had tried to scream but had found myself incapable of uttering a sound. The agony of the effort had awakened me. Now, in my dream, I decided that the simplest way of escape from this expectant audience was to wake up. Yet I felt a sense of undeniable obligation to them. I had come to say something, and they were waiting to hear it. But I could not remember the words. I stood as motionless and breathless as one does when he is about to sneeze. Then I began to squeak and creak. My dismay gave way to relief. Quichua! I thought. Such sounds as I had never heard poured forth from my mouth, and suddenly I awoke. The sound went on, and my mind groped to identify it. A donkey. That must be what it was. I had never heard a donkey bray, but the squeaking and creaking were followed by a recognizable hee-haw, and then I heard the lash of a whip, the clanking of water cans and an angry shout. The donkey clopped down the road and I opened my eyes.

My own bedroom, in my own house. Indi Urcu. My
mission station. I stretched my feet toward the corners of
the bed, luxuriating for the first time in over six months in
its comfort. It was my own, not the short, squarish Ecuadorian one I had used in Ambato. There was no one
waiting breakfast for me. There would be no Spanish
lesson today, no journey, no more half-unpacked living. I
could settle and take possession of the whole house. I had a
whole day before me. In fact, I thought, as I jumped out of
bed, the whole town was mine now, and the Indians. A
promising task, a life's work. Through the window I could
see the valley shining in the sun, mist rising above the
rooftops of the village, and the Indians trotting by on the
road. Always trotting—one leading a donkey, one pulling
a pig tied by a leg, women with great nets full of clay
pots, men with straw mats in rolls on their backs, towering
loads of fodder and corn and hay. They were all in a
hurry, and I felt that I, too, must hurry to meet them. I
dressed quickly and flung open the front door, prepared to
shout a glad greeting to the world. My enthusiasm was
tempered when none of the passing Indians lifted his head
to glance in my direction. Their burdens were supported
by a band slung across the forehead, and they kept their
eyes on the road.

From many an ancient river, from many a palmy plain
    They call us to deliver their land from error's chain.

From rivers and plains, perhaps, I thought, but not from
the high Andes. Not this morning, anyway. Well, I reflected, it's gratifying to see the Indians so industrious, so
bent on the business of the day. I, too, have business—the
King's business—and they little know that it concerns
them.

[42]

Breakfast was the first item, and I found enough food and utensils to make a hasty meal and then set about putting the house in order. Crates, barrels and trunks stood in every room, some of them unopened since that last day in the basement at home when my father had nailed down the lids. Friends and neighbors had come in to help pack, each one wanting a part in a missionary project which originated so close to home.

I sorted towels and sheets—a class of young married women at my church had supplied them, along with a beautiful bedspread, "because even though you're a missionary we want you to have some nice things"—and stacked them neatly in a foot locker in the back corner room which I planned to use as a sort of bath and storage room. The house had no bathroom indoors, but there was a faucet in the kitchen and an ancient flush toilet in a tiny shack at the back. I would buy myself an enamel basin and pitcher for indoor bathing. As I attempted to place some trunks and boxes parallel with the wall, I discovered that no corner of the whole house would have satisfied a carpenter's square. The walls of each room appeared to be approximately the same length, but my boxes sat askew in the corners, and my brain seemed likewise set askew. There were too many doors. Each room opened into two others and I found it hard to decide where I could place a dresser which I did not yet have. I pushed a trunk against the biggest piece of wall in the bedroom and hung a mirror over it. I had wondered, as I packed this mirror, if my having it might be indicative of an unseemly vanity in a missionary, but decided to bring it anyway, unable to visualize a five-year term on the field without so much as a critical glance at my own face.

I pulled things out of the trunks and thought—sometimes with amusement, sometimes with real affection and gratitude—of the people who had given them to me. A case of insect repellent and six embroidered dish towels from an old-maid schoolteacher who had taught me when I was in the third grade; a parka from a man who had once done some climbing in the Andes in Chile, and a pith helmet from a group of Girl Scouts who thought that Ecuador was all tropical jungle; tablecloths of all colors, odds and ends of dishes, camping equipment from Army surplus stores, old costume jewelry to trade with the Indians, Bible pictures and flannelgraph figures for teaching Bible stories "in places where you can't speak the language," as one eager Sunday-school pupil suggested; a braided rug made by a shut-in who collected scraps of wool and silk and nylon and tulle and cotton from her friends and worked slowly day after day twisting them into ovals of all sizes. "You'll want something pretty down there for your house. They won't have anything like this in South America, will they?" I had assured her that they wouldn't, and I spread the rug now on the floor of the front room on the right— this would be the living room. It made a bright mottled spot on the rough wood, and I decided that it was not so bad after all.

I went back into the bedroom, realizing that I was not carrying out my work in a very orderly fashion, and began to make the bed. Frances Rogers, wife of the director of my mission board, had written to tell me to bring a bed—if there was one thing a missionary needed after a long, hard day it was a good bed, and Ecuadorian beds were "impossible." I had been a trifle inclined to sneer at this kind of advice. I wanted to identify with the natives; I even wanted to suffer somewhat. But Frances was the wife of my boss, as it were, and I capitulated.

[44]

I took a look at the living room and decided it was hopeless to do anything there until I bought some furniture, so I began clearing the breakfast things from the dining room. A door led outside to the leanto kitchen at the back, and it was inconvenient to have to open the door, go outside, open another door and take the dishes into the kitchen, but it was out of the question to eat in the kitchen. There was no room for a table and it was without any windows whatever. If I closed the door it was like a dungeon; if I left it open it was too cold. There was nothing in the kitchen except a tile wood-burning stove with a rusted iron top, and a very low concrete sink with a single faucet. Everything was in need of an energetic scrubbing and sweeping and scouring, but at last it was acceptably clean and I felt I could properly introduce all my shiny new utensils and set about washing the dishes. I had a bright turquoise plastic dishpan, hot water from the stove and Ivory soap. Mrs. MacDonald had included the soap in her box of supplies, and although it was admittedly expensive I told myself that missionaries were justified in using it after I saw the alternative—dark brown blocks of waxy substance with bits of straw, paper or fluff embedded in them. It would be positively dangerous to use that for dishes. Maybe for laundry, but certainly not for dishes. You owe it to yourself, all the missionaries said, to keep healthy, and I agreed that they had a point; but then, had I a right deliberately to separate myself from the people I had come to serve? If they could use this soap all their lives, couldn't I? Was it legitimate to spend the Lord's money on expensive imports which could only widen the gap between us? Oh dear, I thought, why must life be complicated by such trivialities?

I plunged my hands into the hot, soapy water and began

[45]

rotating the dish cloth, a gift from my niece, a nine-year-old who saved her allowance so that she might help her missionary aunt, just as I had once done. The lonely mission station, the civilized soap; the dark kitchen and the shining pots and pans; the cold tile floor and the hot dishwater—these things jumbled themselves happily in my mind, a nice mixture of mortifications and gratifications.

It was very quiet in the kitchen. I could hear nothing from the street, for a high wall surrounded the back patio on three sides and the house was wedged between two other houses, part of a solid row of whitewashed walls which filled the block.

A patch of sunlight was sliding down the far wall of the kitchen. Indi Urcu, Hill of the Sun. A lovely name, and this morning it seemed to me a lofty, shining place.

> Great is Thy faithfulness, O God my Father,
> There is no shadow of turning with Thee. . . .
> All I have needed Thy hand hath provided—
> Great is Thy faithfulness, Lord, unto me.

I hummed the tune as I went from room to room, jotting down little tasks to be done, things to be bought. Such trivialities had at last become synonymous with missionary work, for I had arrived in "The will of God for my life." It had been a magic phrase, a thing sought after, prayed about and worried over since I had reached the age of accountability. I wanted to shout my achievement from the housetops, but the next best medium of announcement was the prayer letter, which I must mail right away. I took it out of the typewriter, read it over, decided it was quite a good letter, and imagined it being read aloud in missionary meetings ("Here's one from Margaret Sparhawk, our new missionary in Ecuador. She works with the Quichua In-

[46]

dians"—they will have trouble with the pronunciation of that name, I thought). I saw the letter tacked up on church bulletin boards and beside maps of the world, a colored pin marking the little country of Ecuador, a ribbon stretched to a photograph of myself at the side. Over the map a large caption read: "Unto the uttermost parts of the earth."

As I folded the letter and put it into an airmail envelope I thought of Mavis, who would mimeograph and mail out copies for me from Des Moines. She was a secretary who had worked at the Bible school I attended, and had offered to do this for me even though she worked all day and did the cooking and housework for her invalid mother. "The Lord wouldn't let me go to the mission field," she had said, "but He will let me do this much for you. I would count it a privilege to have this tiny share in your work." Bless her, I thought, God bless her! She's probably praying for me even now.

The MacDonalds popped in as they had said they would, their cheeks rosy and their eyes shining as they came up the walk to the front door. They had had a good night with my landlady; she had let them read a portion of Scripture to her before they retired and at breakfast they had given her a Gospel of John and elicited a promise to read it and to keep a watchful eye on the new missionary. They told me that they would drive up whenever they could for a visit, that I should keep my door and gate locked and not open the windows at night; be careful not to walk too fast or too far in this high altitude; wash my hands as soon as I came in after a trip to town or to Indian houses, and not eat any raw vegetables without scalding them first. All these instructions had been given me by other missionaries in Ambato and I listened politely, but a trifle less earnestly than I had the first time.

"Goodbye, Margaret dear girlie," Mrs. MacDonald said. "Remember we're upholding you *every morning*" (she rolled the r's beautifully) "before the Throne of Grace. The Lord will keep you. Write to us."

There were no Indians in the streets as I made my way toward the center of town. They must be already in the market place, I decided, doing whatever it is they come to do. It was a white man's town and I was sorry about that. I wished there were such a thing as an Indian village, with little houses in a circle, where I could live in their midst and be a daily testimony for Christ. But mountain Indians had no such villages. There might be a cluster of houses here and there, but it was not public as a town is public, and an outsider did not simply move in on them. I had read with envy of missionaries in Africa who lived in villages with the people, or in compounds near the villages into which the natives streamed by the hundreds seeking help of one kind or another. Someday I might have their advantageous position, but the first step was learning to know the town where the Indians did their trading.

It was very cold when the wind whipped down from the heights, but the sun shone fiercely when it was still and I was alternately too cold and too warm. The market place was bustling with Indians when I arrived, all of them impervious to the weather, with heavy ponchos and shawls. Nearly every individual, man, woman or child, wore a hat—great wide-brimmed white ones, dark fedoras, misshapen basins, shallow-crowned sombreros; some of them were set at a jaunty angle, tilted toward the forehead, others were crammed straight down to the ears. There were people wearing two or three hats, one on top of the other—perhaps they meant to sell some of them, or had

[48]

bought a hat for a friend and found this the simplest method of carrying it home. Babies wore hats like their parents' or knitted caps. A few women had cloths folded in the shape of a hat, or cloths laid across the crowns of their hats. Some wore cloths over their hair with a hat sitting precariously on top. The throng of buyers and sellers was a dark, moving sea, bobbing with disks and bubbles.

I skirted the crowd, noticing that very few wore anything on their feet. How did they endure the icy dew of the mountains and the clammy cobblestones of the town?

My first stop was the post office, where I wanted to mail my prayer letter. Two of the women who sold stamps in little kiosks said they had no airmail stamps. A third found one with difficulty. "But, señorita, no one sends airmail letters from here," she explained. Mr. MacDonald had arranged for a post office box for me and I found that mail had been forwarded from Guayaquil and Ambato. There was also a notice of a package that could be retrieved from the window. This was not a simple matter, I discovered. First I must produce my *cédula de identidad*, then fill out a form which required a government stamp, and the stamp had to be purchased from another window. There was a line of people at this window, standing humbly waiting their turn. I could see no one behind the grill. I joined the queue and at that moment a well-dressed white man came up behind me, hesitated a moment, and then strode forward to where an Indian stood. The man snatched the Indian's hat from his head and flung it across the hallway, keeping his chin high and his eyes straight in front of him. The act nearly took my breath away and I watched aghast as the Indian stepped silently from the line and the man calmly moved into the empty place. Not a word was spoken, not an eyebrow lifted that I could see. No one, in fact, had apparently noticed. The Indian was a small man with a slope to his shoulders. He wore calf-length white trousers which flared out above his deeply creased insteps, and a ragged poncho of a nondescript dark hue. Bereft of his hat he looked frightened and ashamed, and he crammed it quickly on to his head again, went back to pick up his bundle, and then came and stood quietly behind me. I wanted desperately to speak to him but I knew it was impossible. Perhaps he spoke only Quichua, and if he knew Spanish I dared not use it before so many white people. What, indeed, would I have said? My heart was like a cold stone in my chest and I found that I was clenching my purse till my fingertips were white. I turned halfway around to give him at least a sympathetic glance but he was occupied with his bundle.

When I finally reached the window the man lifted his hands with a circular motion, palms upward, and said, "There are no more." What should I do? I asked. "Come back at five o'clock, señorita. There will be more stamps at five." He was so cheerful, so satisfied in the consciousness of doing his job well that one could scarcely be displeased with him. This was the way things were done in Ecuador, and the sooner I learned to accept it, the easier life would be. I turned away from the window and started toward the street. A woman swathed in black from head to toe laid a gnarled hand on my arm.

"Just a little token of love, please, señorita, for the love of God. Just a little charity for the love of God, I am poor . . ." I groped in my mind for the Bible's sanction as I fished in my purse for what she wanted. "Give to him that asketh thee." A coin in her hand shut off the petition. She murmured, "May God pay you," and walked away.

There was an overpowering stench of urine as I stepped

into the street from the post office. The walls of the building had a number of abutments which provided a modicum of privacy, and this encouraged the townsmen to make use of them. I began to walk toward the little food store I had seen as the MacDonalds drove me through the town toward my house.

Partly blocking the doorway of the store were two glass cases in which I saw rolls, some greenish-colored sugared balls, round white cheeses, and *empanadas*. I went inside. The woman who was reading a newspaper behind the counter pulled herself up and leaned over the worn board toward me.

"*Buenos días*, señorita. What little thing?"

"Various things," I said, studying my list, which I had written in Spanish lest I forget the words for the items I needed. Then I remembered I had not returned her greeting. How many more times would I make this blunder?

"*Buenos días*," I said sheepishly.

The shelves were packed with cans, bottles, packages, many of which bore familiar American labels, but the prices horrified me. Two and a half times as much as one would pay in the States. I eschewed the foreign imports except for a few things which seemed indispensable—a package of tea, a can of instant coffee, detergent and toilet paper. It gave me pleasure to buy the cheap national foods such as rice, flour, dried beans and peas, sugar, butter, cheese and bread. The woman went over to the doorway to measure out the sugar, which stood in a burlap sack with the top rolled part way down. Sacks of grains I did not recognize stood beside it as her display of goods, for the store lacked a show window, or, for that matter, windows of any kind. The open door provided all the light and display space it had.

Over the counter was a large sign which said:

> Goodbye remedies!
> With one of our healing bracelets it is no longer
> necessary to use medicines. These bracelets will
> cure any disease, pain, or sickness. s/100

The woman came back with a sheet of newspaper containing the coarse, yellow sugar. She laid it on the counter and skillfully began twisting the edges together to form a neat, tight package. She saw me reading the sign.

"They are very, very good, señorita. I have sold many of them, and they cure anything."

"Is that so?" I replied. "It is just a bracelet which one wears?"

"Yes. I will show it to you." She went into a back room and returned with a bracelet, a very ordinary-looking cheap plastic circle.

"You must wear it all the time," she said, "and you will find that your sicknesses disappear gradually. Why, my sister-in-law was dying with diseased kidneys. She bought one of these—she didn't have the money but I gave her credit—and she was absolutely cured in two weeks. Absolutely *cured*. I know many who have been cured."

I smiled and assured her that though I was not sick now the bracelet was indeed interesting.

"You are visiting here, señorita?" she inquired.

"No, I have come to live here."

"To *live* here?"

"Yes, if God wills."

"Ah, how good. You are an American?"

"Yes."

"And how is it that you come here?"

"I am a missionary."

"A missionary! Ah, how nice. But you are not alone?"

"Yes, I am alone."

"But—your family?"

"My parents live in the United States."

"Your parents are alive?"

"Yes."

"Both of them? Mother and father?"

"Oh yes. They are both alive, and my brothers and sisters live there, too."

"And they do not mind that you have come so far away?" She looked at me curiously, moving back to lean on the shelves behind her and folding her arms.

"No, they do not mind."

"But—you are alone . . . you are single?"

"Yes."

"Have you children?" The question startled me a little.

"Oh no, señora, I have no children."

"Ay, señorita. Not even one?"

"No, señora, not even one. You see—I am single."

A small smile played in her eyes as she looked intently into my face, then appraised my entire person.

"Ay, what a shame. How sad to be alone. But you are a missionary, no?"

"Yes. I am going to be a missionary to the Indians."

Her hands fluttered and dropped to her sides.

"To the *Indians?*"

"Yes, señora. I have much interest in the Indians."

"But señorita! The Indians have no souls! They are not souls. Do you think, señorita, that the Indians are like the rest of us?"

"I think they have souls. I want to teach them about God—about Jesus Christ."

"They will not learn, señorita. They will never under-

[53]

stand you. It would be better—much better—to teach us. We need to learn. Indians do not need to learn. Only to work. They are like animals, isn't that true, señorita?"

"In my opinion, we all need to learn. But Indians can learn too. They are human beings like the rest of us. They are not just animals, señora. Christ died for them, too, did He not?"

"Perhaps. Who knows if it is so? But then what do they care if He died? They don't go to church. They don't listen to the priest—only to be baptized and married and buried do they go to the priest."

"I hope they will listen to me. I believe God has sent me. He can help me."

"Well, señorita, you are valiant! God doesn't make them listen to the priest, but perhaps He will make them listen to you! Well, may you have good luck. We are here at your service, señorita." She handed me the groceries one by one, for there were no paper bags to be had, and I put them into my basket.

"Until another day, señora, and thank you."

"At your orders, señorita. Until later!"

When I had succeeded in finding a seamstress and a shoemaker, and had bought a broom and some straw mats, I went back to my house. Approaching it on the street, I decided it was an attractive little house with its whitewashed walls and tiled roof, and it was, above everything, mine. When I went inside, it was not really warm, but there was shelter from the dry, cold wind outside, and there was privacy. I put my basket on the table and sat down to read the mail.

"We have put your prayer card with the pictures of you on our church bulletin board. We prayed for you by name last Wednesday night and the pastor mentioned you in his

Sunday-morning pastoral prayer," said a letter from the church secretary at home in Pennsylvania. The rest of her letter dealt with local church gossip and a visiting missionary whose ministry was "a blessing to us all. Ralph Stone went forward on the invitation to dedicate his life to foreign missionary service. Three others stood to say they would pray for the Lord's will for their lives."

The chair I was sitting in, for a foreigner who had known foam rubber and form-fitting construction, was far from comfortable. I shifted my weight, trying to make myself fit the shape of the chair, and tore open another letter. This one was from a college friend. "I can only try to imagine you there at your station, actually beginning on the missionary work you have looked forward to for so long. It must be thrilling. Remember when we were in the Africa prayer group and you thought you were going to Africa? Well, the Lord's ways are not our ways! Praise the Lord!" One from a former Sunday-school teacher: "We miss you here, Margaret, but we are thankful you have followed the Lord. Do let us know what your house is like. It is hard to picture you there, way up in the Andes, alone. May the Lord give you grace and wisdom and strength as you commence your work for Him."

There were some family letters, one of which enclosed a recent snapshot of my aunt, standing under a jacaranda tree in India with a group of eager children at her feet. There was a magazine containing reports of mission work among lepers in India, orphans in Korea, illiterate slum children in Rio de Janeiro. "The Heathen for Our Heritage," read the title of one article. It told of a meeting in Malaysia which Muslims had attended. "History was made that night as between 350 and 400 people turned out to hear the Gospel of Jesus Christ! Beloved, the seed is still growing for we

[55]

receive reports of many people asking questions, coming to the services, and souls are being saved. God is giving us the heathen as our heritage! Pray for us!"

I marveled at the author's assurance of accomplishment, his candid claim to an extraordinary part in God's eternal program. Would I ever be qualified to make such claims? The activities of the day hardly seemed the antecedents of any history-making achievements. I gathered up the empty envelopes and realized I had no wastebasket. I put them in a pile in a corner and wrote "wastebasket" on my shopping list.

The day had come and gone, and the Indians were again passing my front gate, oblivious, returning to the hills of home, their grains and potatoes and fodder exchanged for kerosene, salt—what else did they buy there? Iron plow blades? Cheap cloth? Bread? They were still trotting, the children tagging behind, bearing like their elders burdens of varied sizes and shapes. I watched them go up the hill until their hats were mere specks against the shadowed fields, and longed to let them know in some way that they had a friend in the white man's village. I had had some vague understanding during my stay in Ambato of the distinction between the Indian and the white man, but it was not until today that I realized the magnitude of the gulf fixed between them. It dawned on me, moreover, that having chosen the Indians as my people I was now to be identified with the despised. The white people, who had always been polite—sometimes to the point of obsequiousness—would perhaps come to hate me. Would it be possible to befriend both classes without offending either? I wondered. "I the Lord have called thee." If this was true, might He not lead me in paths that He Himself had trod? The Scripture said of Him that He was "despised and rejected of men; a man of sorrows, and acquainted with grief." Would I shrink from such a calling? No, Lord, no—only give me an entrance with the Indians; let me accomplish what You have sent me to do.

For a long time the Indians streamed back up into the barren, gashed mountains where their homes were. They lived in the cold, scratching a hard living from hostile soil. I could hear the soft padding of their bare feet and the occasional clink of metal or creak of hemp, but few voices reached me. Was their silence hostile or fearful because they were in the white man's world, or were they just as silent within the mud walls of their homes? What pleasures did they know? Was there anything to laugh about in their lives?

I watched a young woman hurrying up the road, her hands nimbly spinning a skein of wool. A baby, wearing a soft felt fedora identical to his mother's, jounced on her back, one little brown foot patting her hip and one hand patting his own hip as he rode in the shawl sling. They seemed contented enough, but what of the baby's future? What kind of life had he to look forward to? And what did the mother know of lasting peace? I had something to tell her, and how gladly she would hear it when I had the chance!

CHAPTER

6

IT WAS surprising how many days I managed to spend getting settled. It seemed that each day was full of little things that could not wait. I could not begin my work until my living routine was established and my house in order, and although I awoke each morning with the thought of going to visit Indian homes, each evening came before the thing was done. During the day I felt triumphant to see the time passing in useful ways, conscious that I was not sitting down and wasting time, but when evening came and I took stock of the day's accomplishments I felt guilty to see that no breach had yet been made in heathenism. Hudson Taylor had made an impact on China, Mary Slessor on Calabar, John Paton on the South Sea Islands, David Livingstone on darkest Africa. Just exactly how had they *begun?* It was strange to find the actual daily doing of missionary work so unspecific, so lacking in direction. "Margaret Sparhawk is working among mountain Quichuas." I could not get away from the image I knew I had projected at home, but here was the other side of the coin. "Working." What does she do? Missionaries wrote of "doing" visitation, of "reaching" people, of "witnessing." I did not need to read any more missionary books, prayer letters, or progress reports in magazines to learn the terminology. I needed to find out what was really basic in the operation, and I went back to the source, the Bible, and read avidly the Old Testament stories of men with a mission. Moses was sent to Pharaoh.

"But Moses said to God, 'Who am I that I should go to Pharaoh . . . ?' God said, 'But I will be with you; and this shall be the sign for you, that I have sent you: when you have brought forth the people out of Egypt, you shall serve God upon this mountain.'

"Then Moses said to God, 'If I come to the people of Israel and say to them, "The God of your fathers has sent me to you," and they ask me, "What is his name?" what shall I say to them?' God said to Moses, 'I am who I am.' And he said, 'Say this to the people of Israel, "I am has sent me to you." ' "

I read of Joshua. God said to him, "As I was with Moses, so I will be with thee."

And of Samuel, who grew, and "the Lord was with him, and did let none of his words fall to the ground."

There was a young sheepherder named David, ruddy and handsome, who had beautiful eyes. And the Lord said to Samuel, "Arise, anoint him: for this is he." And when Samuel anointed him, "the Spirit of the Lord came upon David from that day forward."

There was Matthew, in the New Testament, to whom Jesus said, "Follow me," and he rose and followed. There was Peter, to whom He said, "Feed my sheep"; Paul, whom He struck blind and later led into a life of unprecedented service; there was, finally, the old exile John, to whom God gave the vision of the Book of Revelation, in which He said "Fear not, I am the first and the last."

The God of these men was my God, and if my faith was worth anything at all, I must act on it. I must start out somehow, and the logical place was in the open-air market —why, it was, in fact, the very place where Jesus and Paul had ministered. There I might meet Indians in a casual way, where they expected to encounter white people and would not be on their guard against us. I had already bought the most essential pieces of furniture for my house in a carpenter's shop, but had learned afterward that cheaper furniture was sold on Thursdays in the market. I still needed a couple of chairs, and decided to combine this errand with the more serious objective of meeting individual Indians. In order to do this I rose early as they did. The wind had not yet begun to blow, and the air was cold and still as I left my gate and joined the trotting, spinning, burden-bearing file headed for the village. Great pale shawls of mist lay along the floor of the valley and the snowcaps floated above them, jagged, detached masses, faintly touched by the rising sun. My shoes tapped sharply on the cobblestones by contrast with the nearly noiseless movement of the Indians' feet. A burro tethered to a stake beside the road followed me with his sleepy eyes, slowly moving one ear forward as I passed, as though he recognized the difference between me and the rest of the traffic. Grass grew between the stones in the road and the dew made them of one color, silver-gray in the wetness. In a very short time the sun would dry the stones to desert dryness and the road would be powdery with dust along the edges.

I was not accustomed to the dogtrot, especially at this altitude, and most of the people passed me, wives following their husbands, children—small versions of their parents, for they were dressed exactly like them—scurrying at the rear.

The sun was just slanting between the houses as I reached the market place, an open square almost in the center of town. Along one side were flimsy stalls with white cotton awnings or umbrellas, some of them walled with sheets of cardboard or rusted iron roofing. Brilliantly embroidered blouses and cheap nylon shirts flapped on hangers from the tops of some of these stalls; others displayed plastic tableware, thin aluminum pots and pans, gaudy glassware and old bottles. There were stalls of gorgeous flowers—white calla lilies, dahlias, asters, geraniums, bachelor buttons, marigolds, sweet peas—and stalls selling meat and cheeses. Great garlands of entrails, tripe, kidneys, brains and testicles from sheep, pigs and cattle adorned the front of the meat stalls, and huge limp mounds of bloody beef and pork lay open on the counters, the flies walking unmolested over them. Beyond the stalls women sat on the ground in front of their open sacks of beans, peas, potatoes of every description, and rice. Nearly every woman had a baby, either peering over her shoulder from a carrying cloth, or lying across her lap.

A foreigner was not a common sight in this market, and the women called to me continually, "What little thing, little madam?" ("*Qué cosita, madamita?*" It was a form of address I objected to—somehow the word *madam* with this diminutive suffix sounded incongruous, especially since I was anything but "little." I hoped I would get used to the term—and after all, I realized, the diminutive was merely an affectionate ending—but it never failed to irritate me.) "What are you looking for, little madam? What may we offer?" I smiled and shook my head and kept walking, picking my way through the litter and trying not to get my shoes wet in the unidentified liquids which ran in the gutters. There was a smell of warm blood and fat from the meat stalls, fresh flowers with the dew still on them from the flower stalls, sour milk from the dairy stalls, high fish and fresh fish, frying tortillas and onions, garbage, wet wool and unwashed humanity—all of this mingled with the ever-present stench of urine from the walls of the buildings surrounding the market and from the cobblestones underfoot.

At the far side of the square I could see straw mats, brooms, baskets, and furniture stacked in crazy heaps. As I walked toward them an Indian with a red poncho and navy blue pants partially covered with burlap approached me.

"What little thing, *madamita?* What do you want, señorita?"

"I am looking for chairs, señor."

"Here! I have good chairs, *madamita,* which one do you like? Just go ahead and choose. This one, señorita? Or this?" Eagerly he snatched up one after another and planted them firmly in front of me. Another man ran up and beckoned to me.

"Come, señorita. I will show you good chairs. Come here, come this way, señorita. Come, *madamita!*"

"Just a moment!" I laughed. "I will look at these first." A woman shouted from down the line, "Come here, señorita! Here I have furniture of every kind. Whatever you want, señorita, everything. Anything at all."

The chairs were mostly of simple design, roughly finished but sturdy looking. I picked one up. It was much heavier than it looked.

"An excellent piece of furniture, señorita," the man said, looking up into my face with earnest hope. I thought of him as I had thought of the woman with the toy suitcases, working perhaps in a shop in the front part of his house, turning out the crude little chairs, and I wanted to help him. Then there was the other man, too, and the woman. I saw a problem created before me. Business matters in my own country had been easy enough, for my motives had been simple. Here, however, a project was at stake and I felt responsible to act in its interest. I must convince the Indians, in any way possible, of my good will, for it was not merely chairs that I wanted of them.

There were a few upholstered chairs in the market, constructed on the fat, ugly lines of the thirties, the sides forming quarter circles, the seats too low, covered with coarse cloth in appalling colors. To put one of those in my living room would be a high price to pay, even to promote my end. No, I would stick with the ordinary wooden ones. I walked along and looked at the others, all nearly the same, wondering how I was to choose the person I would please. I asked the prices.

"Sixty sucres, *madamita*," was the first answer, followed by a shout from the man farther on, "I'll give you one for fifty-five." The woman called to me, "Come, señorita. I am going to show you a good chair for forty-five sucres. Come here, señorita."

There seemed to be no other customers and I felt myself the object of everyone's undivided attention. Did they know that I wavered in the decision not because I was trying to decide which chair to buy but which salesman to gratify? I kept walking back and forth, not replying to their calls. I noticed that behind the mats which the woman was selling she had a pot of corn soup boiling on a little stove. A child of perhaps three or four, wearing only a raveled sweater, lay asleep on a pile of rags beside the stove. He held a piece of blackened banana skin in his hand, and his breath came in short rasps.

"Is this your child?" I asked the woman.

"Yes, señorita. *Buenos días.*"

"*Buenos días.*" I had forgotten again. "Is he sick?"

[63]

"Yes, señorita. He has fever."

"Where do you live?"

"Over that way."

"You could not leave him at home?"

"How could I leave him at home, señorita? There is no one to care for him. I have to come to the market."

"You come here every Thursday?"

"Yes, señorita. And I go to other towns for market on other days. That is how I live."

The decision was suddenly simple.

"How much did you say this chair is worth?"

"Forty-five sucres, *madamita*."

"I will give you forty." It was standard practice to bargain, but even as I did it I felt condemned. The woman needed far more than forty-five sucres, even if that were clear profit.

"No, señorita. Forty-five is the minimum. You can see that I am poor."

I gave her the money. Surprised, she looked at my face with gratitude—in fact, I thought, with something akin to love.

"Thank you, señorita. Shall I call a *cargador* to carry it for you?"

"Yes, please," I said, and she hailed an Indian who stood nearby with a rope over his shoulder. He wore a pressed-felt hat with a round crown and a warped narrow brim. It looked as stiff, as heavy, and as weather-resistant as asbestos, and it was a dirty, yellowish white, splotched here and there with darker stains. His hair was cut raggedly just under the level of the hat brim, a poor compromise, it seemed to me, between the white man's style and the Dutch-boy bob of Indians farther north. His face was broad and unlined with a few sparse whiskers on his chin which gave

[64]

him a callow look that did not match the mixture of suspicion and question in his eyes. He wore loose, un-creased white trousers which reached almost to his ankles, and his poncho, which was blue-black, was folded so that the two outer edges rested on his shoulders. Underneath the poncho he had a homespun shirt of European cut, tightly buttoned at the cuffs and collar. I tried to decide if the poncho was what gave his torso such a top-heavy look, or whether perhaps Indians were normally shorter-legged than Americans.

"I carry this?" he said.

"Yes, please," I said, and he silently strung the rope around the chair and passed the leather portion of it across his forehead, bowing slightly as he hoisted the chair to his back. He followed me patiently as I went from stall to stall, my main purchase made, choosing a few small things to furnish my house—a feather duster, a little brass basin with handles, a moss-green, dull-glaze piece of pottery to put on my windowsill. He collected the things as I bought them, finding a place to carry each. Then we started home.

"Do you live near here?" I asked the Indian as we climbed the hill.

"Yes, señorita, over that way." He pointed with his chin toward the northwest. He did not look at me, for his face was bent downward with the strap across his forehead.

"Do you have a family?"

"Yes, señorita."

"Children?"

"Yes, señorita."

"How many?"

Silence. He plodded on slowly, giving no evidence that he had heard me.

"How many children do you have?" I asked again.

[65]

"How many will it be? Four? Four, señorita."

"Four alive?"

"Yes. And a baby too."

"Then you have five?"

"Yes, five, señorita."

"Did you have children who died?"

"Yes, señorita."

"How many?" Perhaps I was being too inquisitive. But what *did* one talk about to an Indian? How was I to befriend him?

"I don't know, señorita."

"You don't know?"

"No, I don't remember. They are born and they die. Or they grow a little, and, sickening, they die. That is how it is, señorita."

We walked on in silence for a while as I thought of this succinct statement of the man's life. That is how it is.

"What is your name?" I finally asked.

"Pedro."

"And your surname?"

He glanced at me through his eyebrows. If only I could get through to him. If only he knew how I longed to win him for Christ. He had probably had little experience of white foreigners, but his knowledge of other whites had made him suspicious. He regarded them as his enemies, people who were determined if not to destroy at least to exploit him. Since I was, furthermore, a woman, there was little hope that he would believe in my attempt at friendliness.

"Do you have land, Pedro?" I decided to forget the question about his surname for the time being.

"Yes, señorita."

"Do you grow things on your land?"

"Yes, señorita."

We had arrived at my gateway. I was reluctant to part with him without some hope of seeing him again.

"Does your wife ever come into town?"

"No, she takes care of the house."

I opened the gate and he put the things down in the front yard.

"There, señorita." I gave him three sucres.

"*Gracias,* señorita." He turned and went out. I watched his broad short back as he shuffled down the street.

Was this the contact I had set out this morning to make, or had Pedro and the others to whom I had spoken merely slipped through my fingers? I had pictured myself, Bible in hand, against a backdrop of high mountains, talking—*dealing* was the word used by evangelists—with an Indian. Sadly I thought that this was how my praying friends pictured me, too, and the picture was not a true one. Things were just not working out quite as expected. What would I not give—O God, what would I not give—to make the picture come true? But perhaps I am impatient, I thought, as I went into the kitchen to make some coffee. I had, after all, found a nice chair, and that was one of my objects. Not the most important, of course. God forbid that visible things should mean more to me than invisible, but on the other hand I should not overlook tangible answers to prayer. If God had guided me to the right furniture there was reason to hope that He had guided me to the right man, the man who might eventually become a believer and be willing to help me with the task of Bible translation. My hopes leaped ahead and I saw already Pedro's face, lit with joy, reading the Scriptures in Qui-

chua. But it will take a long time, the MacDonalds had said.
It is no easy thing to get next to the Indians. Perhaps I was
taking too much for granted. Perhaps I had frightened
Pedro by asking him so many questions. Well, the Lord
could overrule that, too. I must tread softly. It was like
putting salt on a bird's tail.

THERE WAS an unexpected sameness in the weeks that followed. It was unexpected because I had pictured a nice sequence of events which would visibly mark the progress of the new work among the mountain Quichuas: Getting acquainted, Visiting, Contact, Witnessing, Conversions, Translation of the Bible. Oh, of course I had not expected all this in a short time. It would be slow, but it would, once it got started, be steady, and there would be things to report. Instead of this, things seemed to have come to a standstill as soon as I had met Pedro, and I found myself getting up in the mornings, reading my Bible and praying, eating breakfast and swallowing my vitamin pills, washing dishes and dusting, thinking of excuses to visit as many shops as possible in order to engage the shopkeepers in conversation, going to the post office to get my mail, strolling through the market in hope of making the acquaintance of more Indians, and wishing for something to happen. If nothing happened, where was my *raison d'être?* It was not that I was lonely or bored. Quite the contrary. I loved the setting—the little house, the quiet street, the bustling village, the gorgeous valley and mountains with the big sky overhead. I loved watching the life of those around me, trying to understand what they did and why they did it. But what right had I to enjoy myself if that was all I could do? The world was full of people who had no other aim in life. My very contentment became a rebuke to me. Here were these souls all around me, busy with occupations and preoccupations in which I had no part, and not one of them yet won.

When I was in college there was a red-haired girl with a beautiful voice who sang,

> Over the ocean, millions I see,
> Fettered in bondage, beckoning me.
> Crushed beneath sorrows, too heavy to bear—
> Gladly I answer, Lord, send me there.

The words always stirred me and I was puzzled to find fellow students unmoved by the song, or by the statistics presented to us of the numbers who die daily without Christ. Words like "apathy" and "complacency" ran through my mind and I wondered what such students would have to lay at the Master's feet. There was another song about "nothing but leaves" which came to mind then. Here I was now, over the ocean, surrounded by the beckoning millions, but their lives went on as usual. I saw in their faces sadness and the emptiness of despair at times; I saw poverty and suffering and injustice. At the same time I saw that the sun shone on their peaceful valley and the women spun with their skillful fingers and carried their plump, contented babies on their backs; the men drank firewater in the market place and laughed loudly and ate their potatoes and fried pork skins with gusto, and at evening everyone had a house to go to and the next day would be the same. Once I was on the point of approaching a woman whose face looked especially sorrowful. She was standing beside a display of shoes made out of rubber tires. Just then a man leaned out of a truck and shouted, *"Hola, bonita!"* and the woman laughed and shouted back at him and then turned and gaily swatted a child who ducked past her into the stall. How, exactly, was I supposed to interrupt their lives? If one has been summoned to loosen fetters where does one begin?

Daily I prayed that the Lord would lead me to the ones I should speak to and it seemed on several occasions that my prayer had been answered. I found a woman in one of the meat stalls who could read. She was not strictly an Indian, but belonged to the *cholo* class, of mixed blood, and had had several years of schooling. Since she was there every day I decided to buy my meat from her and concentrate some effort on winning her friendship. She was unusually friendly and interested and after two or three conversations she asked if I would give her a Bible. I hesitated to start out with a whole Bible and suggested that she read a portion such as one of the Gospels, and then we could discuss it and, if she wished, I would give her more. She gladly accepted the idea and each time I went to her stall I found her with the book. She was, in fact, so avid in her reading and so instantaneous in her agreement with all I said about the Gospel that I could not help suspecting that she was only seeking to satisfy a customer. How was one to know?

There was a little girl, too, who begged me for one of my pretty books and ran eagerly home to show it to her mother. She told me later that her mother had beaten her for bringing the foreigner's book into their house and had torn it out of her hand and thrown it away, but the child retrieved it secretly and was reading it. An Indian boy had come to market one day with a small pig to sell. Seeing me sitting on a bench he came over and began to ask questions

[71]

about my books so I read to him and we talked of many things. But when I asked what he knew of God he was frightened and hurried off to sell his pig.

Pedro was often in the market place with his rope slung across his shoulder, and though he was naturally very reluctant to recognize me at first—my friendliness baffled him utterly—as time went on he summoned the courage to answer my greetings. I asked him again if his wife ever came to market and he said that she would perhaps be coming the following week. I tried to find out what day but he only shook his head and said that he didn't know. When she came she would come, he said, using an odd Spanish phrase which I took to be a literal translation from his own language. My faith that God had indeed directed me in the initial contact with this man was renewed, and I sent up a veritable storm of prayer that I might meet Pedro's wife and thereby gain the longed-for entrance into the Indian community. Perhaps she would be my "first-fruits"—for, in spite of the few earlier encouragements, I was still not at all certain that I had ever won a soul.

When I was a student in Bible school the principal had once electrified us by asking how many in the audience had never won a soul. "How many, now," he had said, knitting his brows and leaning toward us over the pulpit, "have *never won a soul?* I want you to stand." The palms of my hands went damp and I could feel the blood rising in my temples. So far as I knew, I had never brought a single person to a decision about Christ. I had tried—not many times, but several, diligently and sincerely, without any result. I stood up. Every head in the auditorium was supposed to be bowed and every eye but the principal's closed. Mine, however, opened for a moment, and I saw only two others standing. Nearly a thousand sat in their seats. I felt marked for life—and even, I thought with horror, for perhaps longer than that. Was I after all one of the damned? At the same moment I felt a loathing for those who ought to have stood and hadn't. Surely we could not be the only three. Yet perhaps we were. Perhaps it was true that of that crowd only three had been disqualified, unusable for God. Self-justification and despair alternated in my mind so that permission from the platform to sit down brought little relief.

Now God was giving me another chance. In answer to my prayer, "Lord, send me," He had sent me and I had every reason to believe that He would glorify Himself by bringing forth results. I went every day to the market during that next week, and at last I saw a woman following close behind Pedro, carrying a basket of vegetables. He eyed me surreptitiously from the side and made no move to recognize me, but I hurried over and greeted him. The woman kept her eyes on the ground until I asked Pedro if this was his wife.

"Yes, señorita."

"It is my pleasure," I said in Spanish, giving my name and hoping she spoke enough Spanish to understand my good will. She smiled diffidently, passed a hand quickly to the mass of gold beads around her neck, and shifted her feet.

"She does not speak Spanish," said Pedro. Good, I thought, for after all if I am to learn her language it is better that we have no recourse to another. Already I imagined myself seated in her hut, scribbling furiously as she talked to me in Quichua and cooked her corn and potatoes. This would be the real beginning of the transla-

[73]

tion work. O Lord, so let it be. Make this woman know that I want to befriend her. Open the door, Lord. Open the door.

"What is her name?" I asked Pedro.

He looked embarrassed. He glanced at his wife; she looked from him to me and back at him. I could not tell whether I had committed a *faux pas* or whether perhaps he could not remember her name. Then, as though with sudden resolution, he blurted out, "Rosa." The effort this revelation cost him made me feel like a thief. I had extorted something from him which he had not wished to give. I remembered that Mrs. MacDonald had told me that Indian women do not take the husband's surname. But I did not yet even know what Pedro's was.

"Rosa," I repeated. "Rosa and Pedro. What is your surname, Pedro?"

He looked sheepishly at his wife, who was watching me closely.

"My surname? My surname is Chimbu, señorita. I am Pedro Chimbu."

"And mine is Sparhawk," I said, smiling. "It is a kind of bird. Does Chimbu mean something?"

"It is my surname, señorita."

"Those are lovely vegetables, Rosa," I said. "Did you grow them?" Then I remembered she could not understand. Pedro giggled.

"Tell your wife that I think her vegetables are very nice," I said.

"*Bueno*, señorita," he said and was silent.

"Tell her what I said," I urged. He laughed nervously and made a move as if to go. Rosa followed and I said I hoped I would see them again. In my heart I resolved to see them. There was something winsome about Rosa's face and sad, humble eyes. If only I could show her that not all white people hated her. If only I could show her God's love. . . .

It took several encounters like this one, widely spaced since Rosa came to market only once a week or less, before I dared to ask the thing I really wanted. In between visits with them in the market I prayed very hard that God would speak to them and cause them to invite me to come to their home. Finally I felt that God was telling me I should broach the subject—after all, He had sent me to them, not them to me, and I should not be shy in the King's business.

I found them contemplating some stainless-steel spoons at a little stall. They talked together for some time and at last must have decided against the purchase and began to move away. I went up to them.

"Buenos días, Rosa. Buenos días, Pedro."

"Buenos días, señorita."

I gave the baby on Rosa's back an affectionate pat or two, asked about their health and that of their children, remarked on the lovely weather, which drew a blank look from each of them, and then asked, "Could I come, Pedro, to visit your house someday?"

He stared at me in wonder.

"To our house?" he said.

"Yes," I said, "I would like to visit your house."

He spoke in Quichua to Rosa. Her eyes shot a hard glance at me, then she said a few words to Pedro, who repeated as though to himself, "To visit our house."

"Shall I come?" I said.

"Come," said Pedro.

[75]

He went with me to the street where I lived, which commanded a view of the valley and mountains, and pointed out the road I was to take.

"When you come to a house, ask them where I live. Tell them Pedro Chimbu, son of Old Pedro. In each house, ask, and they will tell you. They will show you the road."

A LETTER from Woodrow Rogers announced the forthcoming annual conference of missionary organizations working in Ecuador, to be held in Guayaquil in three weeks. It would be well, he suggested, if I would prepare a brief report for my fellow missionaries on the effort that had been started in Indi Urcu. To establish an evangelical work among a million highland Quichuas was our object as a mission board, but to date only three couples were working in widely scattered stations, and now I, a woman, had come. This did not constitute a very significant breakthrough. The Indian work of other missions had been concentrated in jungle tribes heretofore, but the men of vision who had conceived Indians for Christ, Incorporated, saw the immense potential of a harvest among those poor, degraded descendants of the once-powerful Incas and their subjects. Earnest efforts to recruit young men and women for the task had yielded dishearteningly small results so far.

When I read the letter I knew that I must hasten my visit to the Chimbu house. Had anyone accused me of going to visit Pedro and Rosa the next morning as much because of my need of something to report as because of my concern for their immortal souls, I would have been indignant. I rose earlier than usual that day in order to have time to prepare myself in prayer for the task ahead of me. I saw it as a serious task, one on which I had staked my life, and I must not botch it now. The mission also existed for this, and I was their representative. Beyond all this, I was also an ambassador of Christ. He could not fail. It was not simply my own success and reputation that were at stake—it was clearly the success of the Gospel message itself, the reputation of God and all that He had promised in His Word. "For the Lord God will help me; therefore shall I not be confounded: therefore have I set my face like a flint, and I know that I shall not be ashamed." The words from Isaiah buoyed me.

The sun rose and I rose from my knees. After breakfast I put on my coat and picked up my Bible.

The road I lived on ran east and west, and I followed it west for about a half mile, past the last houses in the village and through some fields of corn and potatoes. Indians who hurried by on their way to market did not know that I was on my way to visit Indians. They kept their eyes on the crumbly earth of the road and passed me as though I might have been one of the magueys. You find me here on your road, I thought—a strange figure among your cornfields and potato plants—and you hurry by, resentful, I suppose, at the intrusion, anxious only to escape an encounter and be gone about your business. But when I meet you, I think, Here is one now. Can I catch him? as though I were a hunter. You do not know. You would laugh if someone said, "She has come only because of you."

Jesus once met a woman at a well. She too found it hard to believe that He needed something from her, and even more incredible that He had something to offer her.

[78]

I stopped for a moment to watch an ox pulling a wooden plow through the arid crusty soil. It was hard to imagine that any tender plant could push its way through such earth—pale, buff-colored stuff which cracked into great rocklike clods as the oxen strained with lowered necks and scraping hoofs. "And some fell on dry ground." Where would fall the seed I was about to sow? "Plow the ground, Lord," I prayed as I walked on. "Their hearts will be hard, but You can soften them."

Presently I came to the footpath which ran north from the road toward Pedro's house. It was a dry gully between the rows of magueys, climbing gradually at first and then more sharply, dropping suddenly into a great eroded gash in the hillside and ascending once again the steep slope of the other side. The land was so dry that the dust rose in little puffs with each footstep, and my shoes were full of it. I could feel the cold dry wind stiffening my nostrils and pinching my lips.

A woman passed me, her rigid braid, bound in red cloth, sticking out behind her head like the handle of a pitcher. Her dark blue shawl was caught in front with a long silver pin in the shape of a sword. She threw a dark glance at me and went on, barely pronouncing an *s* in response to my *Buenos días.*

Finally I reached a little mud house, huddled in the corner of a field of grain. It had a steeply pitched grass roof like untrimmed bangs over its one feature, an empty doorway. There was a skinny rooster clawing at the dirt in front of the door, and an old blue enamel washbasin with holes in it lay to one side. I called out a greeting and waited. No one appeared. I called again. Was anyone inside or were they all out in the field? I waited, and then went on, threading the edges of several more fields. In spite of the beauty of the valley and range upon range of mountains, I was conscious only of utter desolation—the sharp cold, the loneliness, the taste of dust, and the fear in my heart. There was no sound whatsoever for minutes at a time. Now and then I could hear the distant bleat of a sheep, and the wind came in choking gusts. I saw another hut, approached, called, and waited. There was a movement near the doorway in the shadows of the interior. I called again, *"Buenos días,"* and a head appeared. A boy with flashing black eyes scrutinized me for a moment, his lips tight, his chin thrust out.

"Can you tell me where Pedro Chimbu, son of Old Pedro, lives?"

"Buenos días," he said. He kept studying me for a moment, then pointed to the northwest. "Over there."

"Shall I just follow this path?"

"Yes. Then when you see another one which goes that way"—he pointed with his chin—"follow it."

"Thank you." I went on, conscious of his continued gaze as I walked up the trail. I could feel his question, What wrong has Pedro done, to be thus pursued by a white woman?

Finally after several more inquiries I reached Pedro's house. It was larger than the others and one section of the roof was tiled. Around it were fields of beans, peas, corn and potatoes, and there was a calf tied nearby and several chickens who squawked at my approach. I called a greeting and after a moment Rosa poked her head out the door. I had the feeling she had long since seen me coming but did not want to be caught watching, so had waited for my call. She came shyly toward me and I smiled, said good morning, and patted her left upper arm with my right hand as women in Ecuador do. Pedro had said she did not speak

[80]

Spanish, but I spoke to her slowly, hoping that Pedro had exaggerated.

"I have come, Rosa, to your house—to visit you. I have come to see you." I could hardly mistake the distrust in her face, but she said, "*Bueno,* señorita. Come," and led me indoors.

I had to stoop low to enter. It was as dark as pitch inside, and the smell of smoke, dried grains, dust and humanity was overpowering. There was a tiny fire of wisps of grass smoldering feebly on the floor. Around it several small animals were moving which I at first feared were rats, remembering the loathsome creatures in Guayaquil. At length I saw that they were guinea pigs. Back in the corner lay piles of sacks and sheepskins, wool ponchos, shawls and blankets. This collection I took to be the bed. There was no furniture in the house at all, but bulging grain sacks were placed about as though they were meant to be sat on, so I looked at Rosa for permission. She waved her hand toward one of them and I sat down, while she squatted back on her heels by the fire and began banging a woven rush fan up and down on the floor to encourage the embers. She set a small black pot on some stones over the little flame. Then I realized we were not alone in the room. Three or perhaps four children—I could not be sure because they were huddled so closely in the dim light—were solemnly surveying me from behind some sacks in another corner.

Rosa was making some kind of drink. She had to keep adding tufts of grass to feed the fire, but she added them very sparingly, inserting them delicately in just the right spots. She said nothing more to me, but spoke in Quichua to the children. The words sounded angry, but the children did not move or reply. She took the pot from the fire, lifting the hot handle with a twig, and set it on the ground. Tipping it quickly with her bare hands she filled two small painted enamel bowls and pointed to one of them.

"Drink, señorita," she said. It appeared to be some kind of gruel. There was so little flavor—not even any salt—that I could not identify it. Nevertheless the warm liquid was satisfying—for one thing, because I was hungry, it being close to noon, and for another, because it represented a welcome from a Quichua woman, the courtesy of an Indian home. I tried to say thank you. Rosa took my bowl and filled it again but offered it this time to the children in the corner. She filled her own empty bowl as well and gave it to them. Was this to be their lunch, I wondered?

When they had all finished drinking, I took out my pad and pencil and began asking the names of various objects, using the Spanish phrase for "What is this?" Rosa looked at me dumfounded. Did I not know a guinea pig or a spoon when I saw it? I repeated the question and she said a word. I wrote it down, using phonetic characters, and the children eased over toward me and peeked over my shoulder at the paper. One of them, a boy of perhaps eight, took the pencil from my hand and made a letter on the corner of the paper—he wanted me to know that he could write. I supposed he had been to school for a few days or weeks, though he looked too small and did not seem to speak any Spanish. At length the children began to answer my repeated question, and made a game out of pronouncing the words for me and laughing at my attempted imitations.

Then the boy who had written the letter said, "*Imatai?*" pointing to my watch. I hoped that he was asking the same question I had asked, "What is this?" in Quichua. I answered with the Spanish word for watch, and he grinned. He tried it again. Pointing to my shoe he said, "*Imatai?*"

[82]

and I again gave the Spanish word. He was elated. He had taught me something.

"What is your name?" I asked in Spanish. His black eyes danced, but he did not reply. I felt sure he understood. "Your name?" I said. "What are you called?"

"Romero."

I looked at the smaller boy, but before I had a chance to ask his name Romero said, "And this one—Jorge." Jorge in turn pointed to his sister, a lovely child who looked to be about nine, but was perhaps older than that. Indians do not seem to show their age.

"This one is Pava," he said in Quichua. I caught the name Pava, and assumed that the rest of the sentence meant "This one is." The word was *caiga*, I thought, so I wrote it down with the tentative translation.

"Pava?"

"*Arí!*" Jorge and Romero said the word in unison, then laughed delightedly. They must have given me the word for Yes. I was pleased with my score thus far.

Rosa went outdoors and the children began examining my coat, shoes, wristwatch, hair and skin. They had seen plenty of white people, but they had not been this close to one. They had learned from an early age to keep their distance from and pay to the white man the respect due a superior. But with the guilelessness of children they accepted my friendliness without suspicion. Life had not yet taught them much about treachery.

When their mother came back inside she placed some leaves on the ground where the guinea pigs could get them and made as if to sit down by the fire. Then she walked over to the bed in the corner and began fussing with the skins and clothing. I tried out my Quichua question on her.

[83]

"*Imatai?*" I said, pointing to the sheepskins. She mumbled the answer so that I did not hear. The children repeated it for me. Rosa was not enthralled by the game and was finding it difficult to entertain a visitor whose vocabulary was limited to a single interrogative. I tried a new tactic. I stood up and sat down, using the Spanish word for "I sit down." It was clear, from Rosa's expression, that she questioned my sanity. I laughed and tried it again. The children watched mystified and delighted, but offered no information. Rosa was at a loss. She said something to me which I did not understand. Several possibilities came to mind: "Are you crazy?" "What is the matter?" or "When are you leaving?" I thought it most likely that she was trying to tell me she did not understand. Well, enough of this, I decided, and resorted to drawing pictures in the ashes on the ground for the children. Still Rosa did not sit down but busied herself here and there doing nothing. Then she spoke sharply to one of the children and the child went outside, perhaps to get the cow, I thought, or fetch water. Their life must go on, and my intrusion was inhibiting the process. Rosa had done all she knew to make me welcome. Beyond that she was at a loss, and my presence confused her. I could not explain my mission and it would be a very long time before I would be able to. But this was a beginning. A visit to an Indian home, a bare beginning on the language—six or eight nouns and a question form; plus the word for "yes." Well, some other day. This was, at any rate, a contact.

I rose from the sack on which I sat, extended my hand to Rosa. "*Gracias*, Rosa," I said. "I will come again some other day." I think she understood the phrase "other day." She smiled.

"*Bueno*, señorita," she said.

I shook hands with each of the children. It occurred to me that Pedro had said he had five children. Here there were three, plus the baby. Perhaps Pedro could not count.

"Until another day," I said in Spanish.

"Until another day," they parroted.

The trail down the mountainside was like broken concrete layered thickly with dust. It had been a mistake to wear thin-soled shoes and nylon stockings, but then I did not own anything else. I would have to see about getting something more rugged. "Sensible" shoes carried all the stigma of the missionary spinster image which I loathed, but I could unhappily foresee my own progressive conformity to this image. Even that, however, could be endured for Christ's sake. "How beautiful upon the mountains are the feet of him that bringeth good tidings . . ." Absurdly this bit of Scripture popped into my mind, bringing a tiny wry comfort.

I stopped now and again to empty the dust and stones from my shoes, and to look at the enormous range of earth and sky spread before me. Never in my life had my eye held at once so much earth and so much sky. I am not very good at judging distances, but it seemed that at least sixty or seventy miles of valley lay before me, drawn up at the two sides like a huge blanket, stretched between invisible stakes where the peaks of the mountains made the horizon jagged. Far to the south the land faded into sky. The colors were muted, with no greens visible except close at hand. The fields were brown and purple and mauve and taupe and gray, spreading to the high country where nothing would grow, where there were only the black of rock, the gray of volcanic ash, and the gleaming white of snow. The lake lay like a silver ellipse far below, and the little village of Indi Urcu nestled, small and insignificant as a heap of pebbles. The sky was a luminous, burning blue, incredible in its clarity. Even the edges of the white clouds seemed sharply cut and superimposed on an infinity. The magueys outlined the fields faintly like strings of dark beads laid neatly and tautly in criss-cross. At odd corners of the square patches huts stood, a few with blurs of smoke escaping through the thatch. The afternoon sun threw a mantle of peace on the whole, and I wondered if I had ever seen such marvelous beauty. Indians passed me in ones and twos, each carrying his unsold wares or his purchases for the day. Their feet were bare—tough, strong-looking feet covered with the dust of the road, with the toes spread as human toes were meant to spread, not crushed and caricatured by the wearing of shoes. Would these feet someday be the bringers of good tidings? The words of Isaiah again . . .

I hurried on down the path. An Indian man was coming toward me, not evading my gaze. It was Pedro Chimbu.

"*Buenas tardes*, señorita," he said. His rope lay on his shoulder. Market would be over for the day, and he would find no more carrying work to do.

"*Buenas tardes*, Pedro."

He asked if I had been in his house and looked pleased when I told him I had.

"*Bueno, bueno*, señorita," he said, looking past me and then at me, as if waiting for my permission to go.

"Until another day, Pedro," I said. "I would like to come someday when you are home. Perhaps you would help me talk to your wife."

"*Bueno*, señorita, that would be a good thing. You come when I am at home."

"I want to learn your language, Pedro," I said, "so that I can translate God's word into it." I hoped this would arouse his interest.

[86]

"*Bueno*, señorita."

What did this reply mean? Was it all I was ever going to get from Pedro? If I did not understand him, he probably understood me even less. Of my declared intention, as of any declaration made by white people, he made nothing. He had never discovered any grounds for dealing with them. Whatever it was they wanted, he was bound to treat them respectfully. I tried again.

"Do you know God's word?"

"No . . . once I went to the church. The priest talked about God, but I did not hear well, I did not understand."

"God has given us a book, Pedro. Did you know that?"

"No, señorita."

"Would you like to hear it? Would you like to hear God's word?"

"*Bueno*, señorita." This time I decided that the reply indicated not a desire to know but a polite willingness to be told.

"Someday we will talk about it. Until another day, then, Pedro."

"Until another day, señorita."

He trotted on up the hill. Well, they aren't headhunters, I reflected with a slight trace of disappointment, for it was beginning to dawn on me that my position among these Indians was not really a very dramatic one. Where the need is not obvious, as it is (it seemed to me) among wild aborigines, sacrifice to meet the need loses some of its nobility. But then, they are certainly godless Indians. (The adjective was a sweeping condemnation, but I used it automatically, having been taught that all were godless whose personal commitment to Christ did not match mine.) They have no knowledge of God's word. What a privilege it will be to bring it to them! I thought exultantly.

[87]

It was said that they had a form of religion, but they needed what I had come to bring, needed it every whit as much as a demon worshiper. Godless heathens, pagan savages, degenerate serfs—they were all the same, and Christ had died for them. Any incipient misgivings I may have had about the effectiveness of my first visit were banished by these thoughts.

Rosa had wished me gone. No matter. Secretly I heaped coals of fire on her head. I was doing her an immeasurable favor, though she was as yet unaware of it. The day would come when she would thank me for what I had brought her. I could look for that day in faith. "My word . . . shall accomplish that whereto I have sent it."

I went on past my house and down to the post office. There was a missionary magazine in the mail and I quickly turned to the South America section. The item was there:

"Miss Margaret Sparhawk of IFC has now arrived at the new station among the mountain Quichuas of Ecuador, Indi Urcu. Pray for her as she begins her work among these neglected people. Pray for help in her study of the difficult tribal language."

I was satisfied. They had me in my slot and could start praying now for the things I knew were going to happen. The word "difficult" made me slightly uncomfortable. I had not used it in my own letters describing Quichua, for I had heard from a noted linguist that Quichua is one of the easiest languages in the world. Well, I thought, the responsibility does not rest with me. If faulty information inspires more earnest prayer, who can regret it?

IN THE three weeks before the Guayaquil conference I visited the Chimbu hut as often as I could, sometimes when Pedro was at home, sometimes when he was not. Rosa was always in or near the house, always working—cooking, spinning, carrying water, carding wool, husking corn—but she learned to accept my coming though she did not clearly understand that her language was incomprehensible to me, or that I wanted to learn to speak it. White people did not speak her language, she knew, but perhaps because she herself had never had to learn it she did not understand why I had to. Was it not perfectly "hearable"? She had certainly not come across a white person who wanted to speak Quichua in preference to Spanish. So my questions and antics, intended to elicit Quichua phrases, she took as a white person's whims, not to be fathomed or challenged. Pava, although she was very quiet and as busy as her mother, missed nothing, her great black eyes following every movement of mine while her hands went on scraping the steel combs over raw wool or beating the dirt out of the tangled piles with a rod. Jorge usually managed to disappear just before I came into the house, but Romero joined in with my work as though it were a game.

"Señorita!" he would call, popping out from under a sheepskin. "Who am I?"

"You are Romero!" I would answer, in Quichua, proud to remember the pronoun and verb form.

"You are Romero!" he would repeat roguishly.

"No, I am Margarita." This required two different forms.

"She says, 'I am Margarita, I am Margarita,' he would chant, mimicking exactly my faulty intonation, for it was no easy thing to forget the English way of answering a question and to reproduce accurately the Quichua intonation. When Romero imitated me, however, I caught the difference, so his mocking proved a great help.

He taught me to count up to ten, but when I thought I had it, he would deliberately confuse me by counting with me and skipping a number. He would point to his foot and give me the word for hand, or to his head and say, "hair." I wished ardently that I knew how to scold in Quichua.

I visited other homes as well, but I had not worked out any plan for covering the territory I called my own—it was far too vast. Any contemplation of a systematic coverage would have discouraged me. I merely set out in whatever direction my mood dictated, having asked God beforehand for guidance to the right places, trusting that circumstances, mood, weather, chance encounters on the road might indicate the ones to whom God wanted me to speak. Long ago, when the servant of Isaac sought a wife for his master's son, his prayer was that the woman of whom he should ask a drink might be the one whom the Lord had appointed. It seemed to me a fairly reliable method of guidance: let the one to whom I speak *be* the one.

Each home I visited seemed a duplicate of the last, and

the Indians themselves hardly differed in their response. They were overawed at the presence of a foreign woman and listened very politely but noncomittally to whatever I said, whether it had to do with the weather or their crops or salvation through Christ. They nodded in solemn agreement and said "*Sí*, señorita," and I knew that some missionaries would accept this as an indication of their hunger for God's truth. Sometimes things worked together happily and I would come upon a man or woman at just the right moment—when he was resting from his plowing or she from her water carrying—and they would be willing to listen for longer than usual. I would bring the conversation around to their need of a Savior and they would agree and then, at such times, I could readily believe that I had been led. More often it seemed that nothing had worked very well and I returned to my house disheartened, feeling that I had gained little either in friendship or in language data. These were the times, I decided, when I had not been led. My faith worked best when things worked as I had planned.

I was to blame, of course, I confessed privately. Two things were wrong—two, at least. I was uncertain as to exactly what I ought to be doing, and I was still lacking in spirituality. I looked forward to the missionary conference in Guayaquil, where I might once more be with English-speaking people and learn from older missionaries how to go about my work, and I hoped that the meetings would provide spiritual fortification.

My vagueness about the course my work should follow made me uncomfortable. I was always sure what needed to be done in my house. It was a pleasure to get up in the morning, cook breakfast, clean and straighten things, shop for food, collect mail, do errands and write letters. It was when those things were finished and I was at last free to do missionary work that I found I did not know just what missionary work was. But of course this is all a part of it, a physical framework for spiritual operations, I told myself. All that one does is to be done "to the glory of God." How familiar the idea was to me. Yet somehow one had to divide it into categories—one could not qualify either for financial support or for prayer support simply by washing dishes in another country. There had to be, besides this inspiring view of housework, a demonstration of deeds accomplished, worthier causes pursued.

I had heard of missionaries' having servants so that they might be "free to do the more vital things to which God had called them," and this sounded altogether justifiable. When I stopped to consider what vital things I would do if I had a maid the answer, surprisingly, was not ready, but I was confident that I would surely find something. There would be some program, some method or means or project I could adopt besides my present pursuit of the language. The real work would begin, I ventured to believe, when the language was conquered—but then, one read of so much that missionaries did without knowing the language at all! I would have to confer with Woodrow Rogers to find out just what the mission policy was. How stupid of me not to have inquired more carefully before I launched out alone! If I just knew the policy . . .

But then there was still my lack of spirituality, of which, God knew, I had plenty of evidence every day. Why, the very evening of the day I had first visited Rosa I had come home elated, praising God for progress, and as I turned the key in the lock a fingernail snapped. Damn it all! was my immediate response, followed by shock in thinking how shocked everyone would be to know that such a word was even a part of my vocabulary. Of course I had not said it aloud—the word was forbidden at home, was not so much as admitted to thought—but I had thought it, and I thought it again when, a minute later, as I was searching for a nail file to repair the damage, the bureau drawer stuck first on one side, then on the other, and suddenly jerked out and dropped to the floor with a bang.

"Missionaries are human beings, after all," was a phrase I had heard, and at that moment it struck me as being so patently ridiculous that I wondered if anyone had ever really uttered it. Human beings! Dear God, what else could I or anyone else have thought? Could we have imagined that they were superhuman, perhaps, or ex-human? People who had turned into something else, subject no longer to human passion and temptation, invulnerable to the ordinariness of living? My mind jumped back to the missionary homes I had visited since coming to Ecuador—the squalling babies, rickety ironing boards, endless discussions of hepatitis and maid problems and customs difficulties. But, I argued with myself, God wants more than this. He offers us something higher and richer, and by His grace I will appropriate what He offers, I *will* be spiritual-minded, even if I am a human being. Now and then my thoughts dwelt on a suitably spiritual level (it seemed easier when I was with the Indians than when I was at home) but I was not the missionary my friends hoped I was, of that I was certain, and I wanted desperately to qualify.

The MacDonalds took me to the Guayaquil conference in their jeep and as we bumped over the roads and ate oat cakes and tea in the grass we talked of the work and I told them about Pedro and Rosa and my hopes for them. They were amazed that I had gotten as far as I had with the Chimbus. "Why, that's wonderful! Why, what a story! It took us months to get into any Indian homes! Oh Margaret, the Lord is good, isn't He? The Lord sent you here!" said Mrs. MacDonald, "and He will fulfill His purposes, for the Indians, and for you, dear girlie."

When we reached the port city they took me to the home of Joe and Jenny Twombley, a couple sent out from home by the same mission as mine, who had recently written to invite me to stay with them during the week of conference. When Joe opened the door there was an odor of fried fish and vinegar, mingled with the steamy smell of clothes being ironed. We went along a dark hallway to the dining room, where a middle-aged woman stood hunched over an ironing board, her cotton housedress clinging to her perspiring back, her hair pasted in wisps to her forehead. The belt was missing from her dress though the loops which should have held it were there. She stopped ironing long enough to shake hands with me when Joe introduced us.

"Guess we're Ecuadorian now," she said, laughing. "We always shake hands!"

"Myrtle works in the Oriente—you know, the eastern jungle," said Joe, "with the Quichuas. You two'll have to get together and compare language notes. Have a powwow or whatever you call it. Here's Jenny—and our future halfback, George."

His wife came in from the kitchen with a very plump, beaming baby in her arms. The baby flourished a spoon with applesauce on it. Some of it got on his mother's hair.

"Oh, Georgie baby, be careful, honey. Come on out in the kitchen, Margaret, while I just finish up a few things, then we'll be ready to eat."

The kitchen was a tiny sort of cave—tinier and darker than mine—with a black sink in one corner and a gasoline pressure stove propped on a packing crate, on which stood the frying pan with the fish I had smelled and a pot of something boiling. Jenny began to bustle around, stirring things and getting out dishes, so I offered to feed George. I was greatly relieved to find that he had been fed. Jenny said there was nothing to do, really, so I went and stood by the open back door, where I saw a large rat sitting calmly in the middle of the narrow patio, nibbling a bit of garbage. He made no move when I appeared. There was a tree in one corner of the yard which threw its shade over most of it, but not a blade of grass redeemed the slick hard surface of mud. The only green besides the tree was the mold which colored the mud.

"I suppose you're used to these rats out here?" I asked.

"Oh yes—aren't they awful? Guayaquil's full of them, but you do get used to it all, I guess." Another one ran along the foundation of the house which backed up to the other side of the yard. Piercing Latin music came from a cheap radio behind one of the bamboo walls of the other house. The volume was turned up full and the music seemed ceaselessly to repeat the same five notes.

"About ready, Mommy?" Joe called to his wife.

"Yes, right away," Jenny answered. "If you'll just take George, Daddy—here, put him in his high chair. Go to Daddy, Georgie. Here's a cookie. Want a cookie, Georgie?"

When the meal was ready, we sat down at a heavy wooden table covered with a plastic tablecloth—the same one, I noted, that had been on the table when I was here before. It was hideous, really. On the first occasion I had viewed it and the heavy plastic dishes and steel flatware as good, practical missionary equipment—didn't I have the same sort of things in my baggage, all but the plastic tablecloth?—but now I couldn't help feeling that they had carried the denial of niceties just a bit far. This downright ugliness—the sticky rice piled in the bowl, the gray-green peas and greasy fish, the careless appearance of the women—was it necessary? Must soldiers of the cross look as though they had just survived a pitched battle? Was this what was required of us?

"Fold your handies, Georgie," said Jenny.

"Fold handies, George, we're going to thank Jesus," said Joe, bowing his head, watching to see whether the baby was prepared to pray. The baby put his two fat hands together and Joe asked the blessing and then began to serve the food.

A child began to cry.

"Oh—Sandy's awake. Will you get her, Joe?"

There appeared in the doorway a child of about three, wearing only underpants, her hair a tangled mat of straw, her face stained and contorted with crying. She kept crying. Jenny reached for her, but she stood on one foot and bawled. This set George to crying loudly too, and the parents tried in vain to quiet them.

"I guess it must be the heat. They've been doing this every day now. Maybe the water. Come to Mommy, Sandy." Sandy stopped crying for a moment, then caught sight of me and burst into fresh yells. Myrtle tried.

"Come to Auntie Myrtle, baby. Auntie Myrtle take baby bye-bye. Go bye-bye, Sandy?"

The two babies screamed, the three adults tried all their tricks. The music outside was as loud as ever, as unremitting. The heat inside was suffocating. Poor Joe and Jenny, I thought. They were kind to invite me, but they had their hands full. I might have done them a favor by refusing their invitation. Well, here I was, and I would try to make the best of it. It was the meetings I had come for, at any rate.

The conference was to begin the next morning, but the regular prayer meeting of the Ecuadorian church took place that evening and I went with the Twombleys.

The church was a square room with unpainted wooden benches and a green concrete floor. The walls were pale green and there was a text printed across the front, *La sangre de Jesucristo nos limpia de toda maldad.* (The blood of Jesus Christ cleanseth us from all sin.) An upright piano stood on one side, an elaborately carved wooden pulpit occupied the center, and at the left was a large piece of white cardboard with a picture of a thermometer painted on it, indicating the progress of a Sunday-school memorization contest. I had sat in countless similar rooms and squirmed on the benches as the congregation sang and the preacher preached—churches ranging from the plain community church in Pennsylvania to country school-houses where I had held services when I spent a year in rural home mission work. I thought now of the blue-and-gray carpet in the first Sunday school I attended, and the brand-new smell of the little low varnished chairs on which we Beginners sat, peeking through our fingers at the patent-leather shoes on the carpet next to our own, and then of marching round the rows of chairs singing, "Dropping, dropping, dropping, dropping, hear the pennies fall, every one for Jesus, He will take them all." I used to ponder just how He would do that. Did He really need them? I was told that He did, in order to get His work done. It made me feel sad to think of God waiting for our pennies. Mr. Lewis was the superintendent, and he always had an "object lesson" for the children. I remembered the glasses of colored water and the padlocks and different-sized spoons and posters and boxes and diagrams of hearts and crosses and crowns and clouds which he used for teaching us spiritual truths. I could not remember much about what those objects were supposed to illustrate. I watched and listened enthralled until he came to the part which began, "And now, boys and girls, this little box is like . . ." Then I would start studying his round steel-rimmed glasses and his tiny, neat mustache, and remember how he looked at his desk in the bank where he worked. My father had taken me in there one day and Mr. Lewis had admitted us behind the brass fence and then into a great, gleaming round door which led to a vault lined with little steel boxes, one of which belonged to my father. To have been permitted to pass that monstrous door seemed a very great thing to me, and I stood hushed in the sanctum, wondering why he had not told us about this round door instead of about cardboard boxes.

In the next Sunday school I attended, my teacher began each class by hissing, "All right now, girls, le's jes' have a word of prayer." I remembered nothing of what she taught us but could not forget the grammar she used. ("Oncet I read about a clock that all the works into it was made outen wood.") But she was, I understood, a "faithful soul," and I was therefore expected to listen to her Sunday after Sunday.

It was the missionaries who spoke on special occasions in these Sunday schools to whom I listened with close attention. They told us about teaching little black or red or yellow boys and girls about Jesus. They taught us to sing "Jesus Loves Me" in half a dozen languages. I responded to the appeals they made, and dreamed of sailing to some far-off land where people waited under palm trees, straining their eyes toward the horizon until I should arrive to tell them what they longed to hear.

It was now long past the hour announced for the beginning of the prayer meeting, but only a dozen people had gathered. An old man opposite me at the back was reading a small New Testament, holding the book close to his eyes and moving his lips slowly. Several women with their hair in braids were talking in low tones. A young couple and a few children made up the rest of the congregation.

Soon Woodrow and Frances Rogers arrived. I had met them only briefly before, but had been impressed with Frances' ability to look fresh and cheerful at all times in so hot and depressing a city as Guayaquil. She looked the same now. She was about thirty-five, plump and neat and self-assured. When she walked into the church her heels clicked lightly and her bracelets jingled.

"Margaret! How *are* you?" she said, coming over to where I sat waiting for the meeting to begin. "Oh, I'm *so* glad you got down to the conference. Well, how do you like it up there? How does this heat seem to you after being up there in those cold mountains? Woodrow! Here's Margaret Sparhawk! Excuse me a minute, Margaret—I have to go speak to these people." She sidled through to the aisle to greet some Ecuadorians, speaking not loudly, for we were in church, but not in a whisper either. Things seemed to be quite informal.

A few more minutes passed and a gray-haired missionary lady arrived whom Woodrow introduced to me as Miss Blake. She did not take time for more than the formalities of greeting me, and then went to the piano and began to leaf through some gaudily colored paperback chorus books before she began to play. The sustaining pedal on the piano was not functioning. She struck the keys briskly, as though they were the heads of naughty schoolboys which needed rapping, and the plink-plunk of the chords had a curious honky-tonk quality, even though I recognized the tune as one we had sung in English at a Bible conference, "The Whole Wide World for Jesus." She played with great earnestness, nodding her head up and down, as she looked first through her bifocals at the music, and then down at her hands.

A few more people straggled in and sat down diffidently as close to the back as possible. Then a door at the front opened and three men emerged—two short Ecuadorians dressed in black suits and black ties, and Woodrow Rogers, tall and bony and dressed in shirt sleeves and a bright bowtie. They went up the three steps onto the platform and the younger of the Ecuadorians stepped to the pulpit and began to speak in a very loud oratorical tone. There was a rustle of hymnbooks, Miss Blake thumped a brief introduction, and the congregation began to sing. This was followed by a prayer, led by the older of the two nationals. His voice rose and rose, then fell in little swoops till it reached the amen, in which several members of the audience joined him aloud. There was an audible sign, a soft scraping as feet were rearranged, another rustle of hymnals. There was a second hymn, a third, then the announcements and offering and finally the preaching, the same routine followed in every church service I had ever attended.

The speaker took a long time finding the place in his huge Bible. He cleared his throat, looked out over the sparsely scattered audience, pushed his glasses down on his nose in order to look over the rims, surveyed the audience once more, cleared his throat authoritatively, and turned his eyes down to read through the glasses. He read a few verses and then spoke, gesturing widely with both hands, slapping the Bible now and then, adjusting his glasses, pointing skyward and then at us, pausing to find his place in the Bible again, turning over a leaf of notes, emphasizing with great clarity every consonant in the name *Cristo*, pronouncing it as though it were an indictment on his listeners. There. He was finished. The Gospel had been preached. There followed a period of prayer which was open to the floor and all of the adults present took part, all of them alike intoning their phrases as the men on the platform had done, everyone joining in to put a period in the form of an amen to each prayer.

Woodrow was asked to pronounce the benediction and we opened our eyes. The meeting was over, and the people began to move around, speaking to one another, fussing with hymnbooks, collecting Bibles and purses. Most of them smiled and offered their hands to me as they passed. I said, *"Buenas noches"* and *"Mucho gusto"* and waited for Joe and Jenny, who were talking with the Rogerses. Myrtle and Miss Blake had their heads bent together over a large folder which looked like a Sunday-school lesson manual. Myrtle looked up.

"Hello, Margaret. Come and meet Miss Blake."

"Yes—we met just before the meeting."

Miss Blake put out her hand. "I didn't shake your hand, though. In Ecuador we always shake hands." She smiled at me, revealing yellowish but original teeth. Her handshake was very firm and brief. "We're glad to have you with us. Where is it you're working?"

"With the mountain Indians—not far from Waira-pamba, where the MacDonalds live."

"Well, that's a needy field. A *very* needy field. You'll

have to learn Quichua, you know. That's the first thing you'll have to do."

"Yes, I'm very much hoping to find an informant to help me."

"Miss Blake has been in Ecuador for thirty-seven years, haven't you, Miss Blake?" Myrtle said. "She worked with national pastors here in Guayaquil for some time, visiting homes and jails and handing out tracts and teaching Bible classes in some of the believers' homes. Now she's in Riobamba."

"Riobamba's a needy field, too," said Miss Blake. "I do the same sort of work up there, but there's a lot of opposition. A lot more than there is down here on the coast. This is a modern city, more open and tolerant. But we have some wonderful opportunities in Riobamba. Praise the Lord for that."

Joe and Jenny were ready to go, and I went with them, pondering what might be the true nature of the work of God.

THE OPENING meeting of the conference was a devotional one in the morning. I stood with Jenny in the back of the church where we had attended prayer meeting, waiting for Joe to come and the meeting to begin. Missionaries of every size and shape, and of as many doctrinal persuasions as could be admitted among those who call themselves evangelical, poured through the door past us.

"Hazel! How are you? You cut your hair!"

"Hi, Harry pal. Whendya get down?"

"Stay here with Mother, Betsy; hold Mother's hand. Betsy! Stay here, I said. We'll sit down in just a minute."

"Well, praise the Lord, Mike, that's just what we've been hoping for. Wonderful. Just wonderful. Right in the main plaza? And they didn't bother you at all? Last time we tried to hold a meeting there we got rotten tomatoes. Say, I'd like to go back there and hold a campaign with you!"

"It's the most delicious stuff. I have the recipe if you want it."

". . . told her that was *not* what I meant but she went right ahead and *wrote* to the director . . ."

I would have known they were missionaries almost anywhere, except for a few who didn't quite fit the pattern. They were solid, serious, earnest types for the most part, the young men with a certain eager stretch to their necks, the older ones with a weariness around the eyes and a droop to the shoulders. The women were pale—make-up was worn timidly by a few—and most of their hair styles were several years out of date. They came in self-consciously, gently shoving their children before them, looking around for a place to sit near the back. Jenny introduced me to a few who stopped to speak to her.

"Margaret Sparhawk? Oh, you're the new one with the mountain Indians now, aren't you?"

"Oh yes—with IFC, aren't you? How do you like working with the Indians?"

"How is it up there—pretty rough, huh?"

My answers to these and other questions were not very articulate. Fortunately the people did not seem to expect answers.

I began to glance over some of the literature spread out on long tables on either side of the door. The titles revealed how other missionaries felt about their calling: "Latin America, Land of Opportunity for Christ," "What Is the Church's Responsibility to Lost Tribes?," "Is God Calling *You?*," "How to Know the Will of God for Your Life," "Ecuador in Her Hour of Crisis," "The Unfinished Task," "The Unreached Millions," "The Great Commission and You." Such themes, in my college days, represented the kind of attitude toward which I aspired. Now as I read them over, glancing now and then at the people who came in the door—people whom the tracts had recruited—I knew that the attitudes represented were no longer to be merely aspired toward, but ought indeed to be mine at this moment. *Were* they mine?

[104]

"So I said to her, I said, 'Why on earth didn't they put you in a place where . . .'"

"Bill—see you after this meeting for the board conference, O.K.? Right in back of the Sunday-school room."

"Sandy!" This time it was Jenny speaking. "Sandy, you come straight back here. . . . Well, why didn't you say so sooner? The meeting is almost going to start. Oh Margaret, would you hold George while I take Sandy . . ."

The pianist—it was Miss Blake again—struck a few determined chords, executed several runs, and the speaker and song leader took their places on the platform. People hastily found seats and the meeting began, following the same pattern as the prayer meeting on the preceding night —Scripture reading, prayer, and a devotional message from the Reverend Ira J. Perkins, pastor of a large church in Toledo whose Gospel broadcasts had collected a great deal of money for missions in Ecuador. Ecuador was his special project and Mr. Perkins plugged it whenever he had the chance. He was introduced by the chairman of the largest mission board represented at the conference.

"We all know what a blessing Mr. Perkins' broadcasts have been to us—back home in the States and here by short wave—so we're looking forward to a time of real blessing here together this week, with him and with the Lord. Mr. Perkins, we're glad to have you."

Mr. Perkins was a small man with a very powerful voice. He began by telling us what a privilege it was to be a missionary to the missionaries. Then he told one or two humorous stories and proceeded to speak about bearing fruit for Christ, using the fifteenth chapter of John as his text. "The secret, beloved," said Mr. Perkins, "is to abide. Abide in the Vine. Christ is the Vine. Just abide. Now isn't that simple? You and I get so busy running here and there,

[105]

doing things for Christ, trying to serve the Lord, when all He tells us to do is *abide*." He explained in careful detail how the branches abide in the vine, and left me wondering, as I had wondered all my life, what Jesus had meant by the word *abide*. The secret that Mr. Perkins had set out to divulge was still a secret to me.

"Good message, wasn't it?" I heard afterward. "My, that was a blessing. You get so dried up on your station, it's good to hear something like that. Take in for a change instead of always giving out—you know what I mean."

Then there was a coffee break, called a "Fellowship Hour," during which everyone seemed elated and busy and said the same things over again to one another. I did not find much to say to these people, and spent the time standing with a cup of coffee, trying to overhear others' conversations. "Our work" and "our mission" and "our Indians" and "our tribe" were phrases I heard again and again. They all seemed to belong, they knew the lines, and they wore—I must be imagining it—the same masks. All carried well-worn Bibles, the men large, dog-eared black ones with overlapping Morocco covers, the women smaller ones, some of them with colored bindings, some with names engraved in gold. I noticed in the coffee hour something that had escaped me when I watched the men coming into the church before the meeting. There was a hail-fellow-well-met spirit among them here, but they seemed to see only one another; they acknowledged the presence of women, but without looking any of them straight in the eye. The women on their part—young, pregnant wives, single women with hope in their eyes, overweight older ones, attractive and unattractive—looked as though they had sacrificed much for the cause of Christ, and, stabbed with shame, I thought, Who am I to be their judge? God looks on the heart.

There were certain shades of distinction between members of different mission boards. There were boards which forbade their women to wear make-up, boards whose members were vegetarians, boards which drew their recruits from among midwestern farmers and boards which required attendance at the same Bible college, boards which had a preponderance of single ladies and boards whose members had been born, nourished and cherished by a single denominational group and had survived only by conformity to that regime. I had once heard someone remark that a missionary could be the laziest or the most overworked person in the world. Here I saw both kinds.

Suddenly I felt an overwhelming claustrophobia. It was not only the heat that stifled me. Finding myself inextricably packaged and labeled in the same box with these who bore their labels, it appeared to me, so easily—not to say proudly—put me in a state almost of panic. Someday, God willing (but suppose God willed and I didn't?)—at any rate, someday by the grace or something of God, I would fit into the box. Someday the label would justly apply to me, but not yet. Definitely not yet. I did not meet the qualifications, I could not pass inspection, certainly I was not up to the standards declared on the label. There were still far too many contradictions within me. Perhaps this conference would have some salutary effect.

The next meeting was a series of reports from representatives of the various participating missions. Again it began with a hymn—just two verses, the first and last, of "Send the Light"—and a brief prayer in which the leader asked the Lord's blessing on our gathering together this morning, "that everything might be done to Thine honor and to Thy glory, in Jesus' name, Amen." It was so predictable to me that I hardly had to listen, and caught myself examining the shading of the letters on a motto which had been strung across the front of the room: "All Power Is Given Unto Me." The lettering was neatly done, in gold with red shading, like the motto which arched over the minister's head in my little home church. He had stood, as it were, on exhibit before the words "My tongue shall speak of Thy Word." All that his tongue had spoken had fled from my memory but the claim remained, a convincing label.

Eleven American and two British mission boards participated in the annual conference. A spokesman for each gave a survey of its work and the achievements of the past year. We heard first about evangelism among children of the coastal cities. Four hundred and twenty-three Bible club meetings had been held in churches, homes, stores, and on public plazas. Several thousand Scripture portions had been memorized by the children, four children thus winning a free week at youth camp—they had memorized entire chapters of the Bible. A number of incidents were recounted of the children's having been punished for attending meetings and then of their having won their parents to Christ in the end.

A thin, handsome, well-dressed man told of radio broadcasting in fourteen languages. The Gospel was being given out over the air waves night and day—with cultural programs in between, of course, along with news reports and music—and letters poured in daily to tell of blessings received. "A microphone ministry is not always an easy one—it can be deadening. Pray for us, that the quickening power of the Holy Spirit will anoint each broadcast as it goes out, reaching into homes of people who would never darken the doors of a church."

Then a stocky, red-faced missionary from Nebraska told about importing pure-blooded bulls and a special breed of rooster in order to help the mestizos who live in the lowlands to improve their cattle and poultry. "God can use a thousand methods to get people to listen to the Gospel, and if we can help them physically—they sure need it down our way—then they're more likely to listen to the preaching on Sundays. We have two classes a week for farmers, when we give them instruction on fertilizers and feeds and breeding and things like that, and then at the end we have a little message from the Lord for them." He told of three who had come to Christ through this means, and had found farming more profitable since their conversion.

A missionary from the eastern jungle gave statistics about the numbers of tribes and the probable number of people in each. "Of course, nobody really knows—they haven't made a complete census. We're working in three of the tribes . . ." and he went on to tell of baptisms in jungle rivers ("The crocodiles never seem to come around when we're baptizing somebody. Guess even the devil keeps his distance—for a while anyway!"), schools for Indian boys, prenatal clinics for Indian mothers, snakebite cases successfully treated, portions of Scripture translated into Indian dialects, even a witch doctor who had been converted and insisted on turning over his fetishes to the missionary.

A member of another board reported on their work in a different section of the jungle—schools, clinics, churches, even literacy classes for adult women who until now didn't want to learn to read. "In fact, the men didn't want them to learn for a long time, but now they are loosening up and letting their wives come to classes, so we praise the Lord for this step. One of the younger women has actually been helping my wife in the translation work, an unheard-of thing only a year ago. So pray for the jungle Indians. Scripture says there will be some from every tribe and nation, and we believe God has called us to work with Him toward that end."

"All power is given unto Me." I looked at the words again behind the speaker. He was talking now about the distribution of tracts in market places in the sierra cities. Of the thousands scattered like seed (and here he spoke of the prodigality of nature: "Think of the seeds God wastes!") there were a few examples of fruit, that is, souls saved because of having picked up a tract. "For every thousand thrown away, if we win one soul it's worth it! Amen? *Amen!*" And most of the congregation seconded it.

The chairman closed the meeting with a plea for more concerted prayer for the work which was going on, and for more laborers to be "thrust into the harvest fields."

"Truly," he concluded, "as we look about us in this great field of opportunity here in Ecuador, we see much land yet to be possessed, and the laborers are few. May God give us purer, more dedicated hearts, and a real burden of prayer."

He and the others who had spoken used a language and a distinctive tone that echoed through my mind from a thousand pulpits, pulpits of plain wood, carved wooden pulpits, painted pulpits, but each of them the dais of like men, men who with a notable facility and sameness of phrasing could present what was called the missionary challenge. I had never thought of these phrases as platitudes, and I did not question what they had to say. Like the primitive tribesman who, upon hearing a recording about God, was convinced of its truth because it said the same thing each time it was played, I accepted what they told me as true. It was supported, I believed, by Scripture, and I took it as the voice of God, quite unaware at the time that it little moved me. I deplored, in concord with the preachers, the coldness of my own heart. I capitulated to their arguments that the deficiency of my missionary work now must lie in my own lack of prayer, my failure to surrender to the Lord, and my imperfect apprehension of the power of the Holy Spirit.

"Shall we bow in prayer?" said the chairman. We bowed, and there was a cacophony of coughs and throat clearings.

"Our Father, we thank Thee for what we have heard this morning about Thy work here in Ecuador. We thank Thee for what Thou hast done in this beloved little country, through those who have given themselves to Thee for Thy service here. We ask that Thou wilt bless each work here represented. We pray especially for the believers in each area, that Thou wilt make them strong Christians, faithful to Thee in the midst of temptation and the pull of the old life and its associations. Be with each of the missionaries and guide them in their future service for Thee. Give us a renewed vision of what it means to serve Thee and a deeper burden for souls in Thy great harvest field. May we go forth from this meeting refreshed and strengthened to serve Thee, for we ask it in Jesus' name. Amen."

There were to be separate meetings of the various mission boards during the evening, and I was expected to present my report to the session of Indians for Christ. I spent the afternoon preparing for this. It was quiet in the house while the others were taking their siestas, but concentration was difficult afterward. I went over and over what I had seen and heard in the morning. What could I say to match that kind of success story? What *was* there to say? There was no point in getting panicky about it—after all, there would only be a few people, it would be informal, and obviously they were not going to expect much from a newcomer who had only been working a few weeks on a station. Just tell them about the situation—the ideal location for my house, the thousands of Indians within an hour's walk, the contact with Pedro and Rosa, the beginning on the language. What else would they want to hear? It was very simple, really, and something to praise the Lord for.

It was stifling in the dark little room. The house was long and narrow, and the central rooms had no windows at all, though the ceilings were exceedingly high. I thought of my own little house with its small, cold rooms and its sunshine and red geraniums, the wind whipping around the corners at times, the deep silence at other times. George cried off and on during the afternoon and I could hear Sandy's piping "Mommy!" up and down the hall. I would have given a great deal for some of Indi Urcu's solitude. The general atmosphere of this house was one of confusion, as though the whole family had just arrived from somewhere and had not yet unpacked. It was like that a year ago, too, I recalled.

But for this evening I had been invited to dinner, along with a Dr. Lynn Anderson, to the Rogerses'. Frances had introduced me to Dr. Anderson during the coffee hour and, now that I looked back on it, there was something distinctive about her, something—could I call it reality?—which made me look forward to the evening.

CHAPTER

DR. ANDERSON arrived at exactly the hour she had specified, impeccably groomed in a dark cotton dress of simple cut, her ash-blonde hair drawn back carefully in a bun. She wore Ecuadorian earrings of hand-wrought silver with a bracelet to match. I noticed that her car was well polished.

"Well," she said, negotiating smoothly a remarkably rough road, "what sort of day have you had?"

"Oh, it's been very interesting, really. But so hot! I'd forgotten how hot it can get here on the coast."

"Terrific, isn't it?"

"Yes, I suppose I feel it more because the sierra is so cold. Is that where you live, too? Where *is* your work, Dr. Anderson?"

"Please call me Lynn, if you like. I live in Cuenca, in the southern part of the sierra."

"Oh, yes. You have a hospital there, haven't you?"

"Just a clinic. I have four nurses and two national doctors who work with me, but we don't have inpatients."

"What mission are you with?" No one had told me Lynn's connections, and as yet I could not tag her in my mind.

Lynn laughed, tilting back her head. Then she looked at me quickly, her eyes becoming serious again.

"Suppose I didn't tell you? It doesn't really matter much anyway, since my connection with the mission is becoming less and less tangible. Besides, I think it's much more interesting to know people than causes and movements, don't you? As soon as you put somebody in a pigeonhole, you want either to endorse him or cross him off. Did you enjoy the meetings this morning?"

"Why, yes. I enjoyed Mr. Perkins' message."

Lynn said nothing. She waited for me to go on.

"And then, it's certainly encouraging to know that there's so much missionary effort going on. I mean, you see such a need all around and it seems so hopeless to do anything about it, and then when you hear all these reports you're convinced it's not hopeless after all."

"And suppose, after a few years' work, you found that it was?" Lynn watched the traffic and did not give me a chance to learn from her face what she meant.

"Oh, but it couldn't be hopeless," I protested. "You don't mean that that's what you've found?"

"I was asking a question. What would happen to your idea of God, for instance, if you found that your work was useless?"

"To my idea of *God?* Why, nothing, I hope."

We had reached the Rogerses' house and Lynn parked the car with easy skill. She must be a very good doctor, I thought, the picture of confidence and efficiency. I saw that she had a certain dignity in her walk as we went toward the front door.

The house was orderly and cool, with the smell of roast beef coming from the kitchen, the table attractively set at the far end of the living room, fresh flowers in several places. Miss Blake was there, dressed in a very bright crepe dress with pink flowers which cried out for some faint response from her gray face and hair. Frances introduced us to another couple named Ernie and Maxine. Ernie was the one from Nebraska who imported bulls and roosters. Myrtle was there, too, sitting on the edge of a chair beside Maxine.

"Strawberries!" said Maxine. "Where?"

"At the market. And beautiful red ones, too—not those gray squishy ones they usually have. I think Point Four has helped develop them."

"How much were they?"

"Only four sucres a box. I didn't think that was too bad, considering what you'd pay in the States."

Ernie lounged in a corner of the sofa, reading a magazine. I could see the title of the story: "Are Christian Teen-Agers Stuffy?"

"Daddy!" came from the children's bedroom.

"What is it, Linda?" called Woodrow.

"Can I have some ice cream?"

"No, Linda, you go to sleep. You should have been asleep long ago."

"Barry had ice cream."

Woodrow said nothing.

"Barry had ice cream, Daddy. Why can't I have ice cream?"

"Didn't Rosario give you ice cream for your supper?"

"Just some. Not a lot."

"Well, wasn't that enough?"

"Barry got a lot. Can't I have some now?"

"No, Linda, you go to sleep. Daddy means it."

"Why?"

"You'll wake Marilyn. Go to sleep, I said, Linda."

"I want ice cream."

"Linda."

"What, Daddy?"

"You know what. Go to sleep."

"Daddy didn't pray with me."

"Mommie prayed with you a long time ago. Now you be quiet."

"I want Daddy to pray."

Woodrow went into the bedroom. There was a low murmur, then a higher-pitched murmur, and he emerged, closing the door softly. He flopped down on the other end of the sofa and picked up a magazine, leafing through it idly as he turned to Miss Blake.

"Not a bad crowd down for the conference, is it?"

"Daddy! Will I get ice cream tomorrow?"

"Linda, you be quiet this minute."

"O.K., Daddy." There was a pregnant pause. "But Barry won't get any, will he?"

"Linda won't get any if she doesn't go to sleep."

"I'm going to sleep, Daddy. Daddy, I'm going to sleep now."

Woodrow smiled at Ernie with one side of his mouth. Ernie shook his head.

"These kids," said Woodrow.

There was evidence of them in the room, though everything was neat. In one corner stood a low square table with a seat built into an opening in the middle of it. There were toys spread on top of this, and under the coffee table lay a small cement mixer. The floor of the room was of polished brown and white tile and the walls were plastered and painted off-white. Frances' good taste showed in the choice of slip covers and draperies and in the artistic arrangement of flowers on the mantel. She came into the room, wearing a small bright apron, carrying a tray of glasses. Woodrow rose and took the tray and passed it to the guests. Ernie, I noticed, did not get up. He found the magazine story absorbing, and looked up only long enough to take the glass of tomato juice offered him and to say thank you. There was no place for Frances to sit down. Ernie did not notice this and Woodrow had gone to the kitchen for napkins. I had begun to get a chair before Ernie came to and took it from me.

As we sipped the juice Miss Blake described her ride to the meeting that morning in a *colectivo*, a cross between a bus and a station wagon.

"They aren't supposed to stop for you unless they have a seat, but it was rush hour and when I got on there wasn't a seat left so I protested and the driver pointed to the little seat on his *left*—you know the one, don't you, Margaret— that little boxlike affair, hardly big enough for a child, on the *left* of the driver's seat. So of course I told him I couldn't sit on *that*, so a man behind him slid around onto the box and I finally got his seat. But the buses are even worse, and it's worth the difference in price, don't you think so, Frances?"

"Oh, definitely. What's four cents?"

"Well, I used to think it was plenty, but after I got my purse stolen on a bus and lost fifty-five sucres I decided even a missionary had a right to ride the *colectivo*."

Rosario, Frances' maid, was putting the food on the table.

"Ya, señora," she said, and Frances invited us to sit down.

"Frances, this roast is perfect!" exclaimed Maxine, when the food had been passed around.

"Oh, I don't take any credit. Rosario does everything,

really. I can even leave the meal planning to her if I want to. Of course, she'd like to feed us nothing but rice and *fideo*." Missionaries, I noticed, had an irritating way of throwing in Spanish words as though they were English. "So I have to sorta help her balance the meals for us. She cooks her own rice and stuff, of course, regardless of what we're having. Without rice it's just not a meal in her book."

"Oh, I know," Myrtle put in. "My Filomena is the same way. I never saw such mounds of starch as she can put away. How do they do it, and not get any fatter than they do?"

"They eat in bulk what we eat in variety, you must remember," said Miss Blake.

"Well, with the diet I'm on now there's precious little *variety*," said Maxine, and from there the conversation went on and on about diets. Then it was the heat, the dishonesty of tradesmen and mechanics, poor gasoline which ruined cars, red tape involved in getting things into the country, the conference and the people who attended it, with their poor Spanish, poor health and poor support from home.

"And the way these nationals think we're all *made* of money!" exclaimed Myrtle.

"You can hardly blame them," said Miss Blake, "when you compare our way of life with theirs. We belong to the upper class, by their standards, and we can't get around it."

"Maybe we should learn to identify more," said Woodrow. "Jesus was a poor man."

"Yes, but then how do you reach the upper classes?" said Myrtle. "Besides, if we identified with the lower classes, we'd be spending all our time doing the things they do, and we'd never get any missionary work done. How could we take our clothes to the river and wash them by hand? Or cook on a wood stove in a bamboo shack, spending all day making all those complicated soups and things?"

"Well, I guess it's been done. Missionaries have had to do worse than that."

"But this is the twentieth century. We've got to adjust to more modern missionary methods."

I was lost. The arguments disregarded, it seemed to me, the principle of renunciation and sacrifice to follow Christ. What were we here for? And yet I could not answer the questions raised in my mind. Someone noticed my silence, and a few polite inquiries were made about my work in Indi Urcu. I described my house and the village and the great need around me, and they all thought it sounded like a great opportunity and were relieved to know that another missionary had come to work expressly with the Quichuas. Miss Blake talked about her work with the little church in Riobamba, a series of small successes which punctuated her continual giving out of tracts and going from door to door.

"But it's so hard to get people at home to see the need. They think of jungle missionaries as the only ones on the front lines. It's so hard to convince them that we who labor for the Lord in the cities are just as much on the front lines, just as much in need of prayer and support. If only I could get a young couple or a couple of young men to come up there and work with me. My, the opportunities!"

The use of the term "front lines" puzzled me. It was not clear just which were the front ones, now that I was in Ecuador. Once I had thought of all missionaries as on the front lines, but now distinctions were being drawn and I wondered how my work would be classified. Lynn saw the puzzlement in my face, I was sure, though her expression did not perceptibly change.

I did not dream of challenging the truth of Miss Blake's statement. It must be quite legitimate to refer to certain aspects of God's work as strategic, but on what basis did one single them out? I could not argue the thing through, but I knew that it made me uneasy to hear her speak as she did. Perhaps I had an imperfect recognition of the loftiness of my calling, a lack of vision which forbade me to assign to the work its full status in the economy of God. I was an inexperienced, immature worker and it ill befitted me to criticize the terminology used by a veteran of years of service.

Frances passed me a basket of rolls.

"Oh, I couldn't, thank you, Frances. They are delicious, though. Miss Blake, will you have one?"

Miss Blake took one and went on.

"It's a real joy to contact some of those young house-wives there in Rio. They're bored and lonely and it's amazing how receptive they are, for the most part, to the Gospel. They hardly ever refuse the Scripture portions I offer them, and who knows how many are blessed by them? Of course it's another thing for them to come out to the services—their husbands or the priests might find out, and they're afraid, but I do give them the plan of salvation, and then, even if I'm never allowed inside the door again, I know they've had the chance to accept Christ. Of course, some of them are hard all right. Only God could ever break through to them—they slam the door right in my face."

There were small pauses after some of these utterances, as though Miss Blake expected assent from the audience, but I had the odd sensation that we were listening to a

recording and consequently need not respond. Finally
Woodrow spoke up.

"Well, I've always heard Riobamba is a hard place.
Wonder why it is those mountain cities are so hard to
crack?"

"I think it's just what I was saying—people don't pray
for them, they're just not as interested in that kind of work
as they are in more dramatic or romantic work. Then, too,
young couples come out, and we try to interest them in
working in the cities, but they're always attracted to the
Indians and there they go."

"I wonder," Lynn spoke for the first time, "if it is
possible that God might have some excellent reasons, quite
outside our imaginings, for not doing what we think He
ought to do?"

"What do you mean?" asked Miss Blake.

Lynn paused, her water glass halfway to her lips. "We
are accustomed to blame the deficiency of missionary work
on our own lack of prayer or failure to surrender, or on
our inefficient methods or the coldness of the church at
home, or even on the hardness of the native heart—the
notorious failure of Christian missions among Mohamme-
dans is often accounted for in this way. . . ."

"Would you deny those things?" Miss Blake asked, her
eyebrows drawing together.

"I question whether they explain everything."

"Oh well, of course they don't explain everything. But,
after all, we have the clear command of God, we know
what His will is concerning the evangelization of the
world, so if it doesn't get done you wouldn't blame *Him*,
would you?"

Lynn took a sip of water. I held my breath. She would
surely say no. What other answer could there be if we

were not to let the whole structure of our faith collapse? Why were we here if God was not going to keep his part of the bargain? Lynn said nothing, but looked from Miss Blake to me, and then to Frances and Woodrow.

"Oh no," said Frances. "We can't explain the way God works, we know that. Lots of things happen that we can't explain. Look at the beheading of John the Baptist. But then in the end God shows us that it was all for the best, and who knows how much greater glory He got because He allowed John to be killed?"

"That's true, Frances," said Woodrow. "But we're talking about the evangelization of the world and the reasons for its apparent failure so far. I see no other explanation than the indifference of the Church. Christ gave the command, Go ye, and if we don't obey, we're responsible. That's all there is to it. The burden of proof lies with us to show why we didn't go."

"Exactly," said Miss Blake. Her eyes darted from one to the other, missing nothing, as though the moral responsibility for the entire group rested with her. "Why, you'd take the whole motivation out of missions if you put it on any other basis. We know God could have done it some other way, but He chose us to be His ambassadors, and woe unto us if we preach not the Gospel." She looked at me almost accusingly, as though I had taken a position on the other side. Not for the world would I have contradicted her or the others. What they said was to me ineluctable. God keep us, I prayed, from human rationalization which cracks the very foundation of our faith.

"Did God," asked Lynn quietly, "ever destroy anything which He Himself had built?"

"No," said Miss Blake without hesitation, "at least not until men had been so disobedient that He had to. But what are you trying to say? Don't you believe, Dr. Anderson, that we're here to win souls? Don't you believe *that?* What *is* the missionary task, after all?"

"I am no longer as sure as I once was." Lynn smiled, a gentle admission of vulnerability.

"Well, we're here to serve the Lord. I don't know what *you're* here for." Miss Blake attacked the piece of meat on her plate. Frances offered us more mashed potatoes and peas and tried to direct the conversation to a discussion of the hopelessness of the Ecuadorian customs system. Woodrow had spent two entire days trying to retrieve a pair of new glasses which he had had sent down from the States. We all commiserated with him, and other examples were cited which proved the system worse and worse, but conversation was strained for the rest of the meal. A few clear pronouncements on one side and a few honest questions on the other had, in a matter of minutes, shown me that life was not going to be as simple, ever again, as I had thought. It was as though, during a stage performance, someone had peered around from the wings, and though the actors did their best to ignore him and then to make him gracefully retire, the play was ruined. The lines petered out in banality.

There was a little time before the session and I wanted to get away alone. The others went to the church, but I decided to walk. I must determine whether anything I had heard at dinner made it necessary for me to revise what I had planned to say in my report that evening.

I went out to the Malecón and walked by the river, too absorbed this time to notice the things that had bothered me on my first visit to Guayaquil—in fact, my general impression this time was that the city was very modern indeed, a progressive and bustling metropolis.

[123]

I was supposed to tell of my work. What was my work? Reaching the mountain Indians, of course. What was my object? Souls. How was I to seek this object? Why, by witnessing, giving out the Gospel. And this, of course, could not be done until I learned the language. That was the obvious first step, and that was what I'd begun to do. There were no texts, no language schools to attend. I must do it on my own. The mission would want to know my specific prayer requests: first of all, my own spiritual needs—a genuine concern for the souls of the Indians, a wholehearted abandon to the task, a willingness to go to any lengths in order to bring others to the Savior. Then I needed prayer for special help in the language, wisdom in knowing how to make contacts with individuals, guidance to those who were prepared by the Spirit of God. That would do it, I thought. That would easily fill my seven or eight minutes; it would be an honest presentation of the work and a good summary of my needs in connection with it.

But the dinner-table conversation kept plaguing me. Lynn's calm questions had shaken me, but Miss Blake's instant answers, which were precisely the answers that had popped into my own head to give to Lynn, shook me even more. It was disquieting to discover now, as I walked by the river and went over the talk in my mind, that what Lynn had said had also been in my thoughts at times and I had not dared to give utterance to it. I had answered myself, at such moments, as Miss Blake had answered Lynn, and had succeeded in silencing the conflicts. They were not so easily silenced now. Then I thought of Woodrow and Frances, kind and generous and anxious to make us all happy; Woodrow, in his position as field director of the mission, obliged to take a certain position while at the same time diplomatically acknowledging the right of another to examine it. I was a member of the same mission. I was committed to the same set of propositions. Just how was I going to blend into this picture? I would have to be careful.

The evening session was as I had expected. There were more reports, detailed this time, sprinkled with "our people," "our work" and "our territory," but the possessive included me this time, since I was a member, so it was my work, my people, my mission. When it was my turn, I said what I had planned to say and sat down, having given no one reason to wonder whether I was qualified to carry the banner, whether I was wholly convinced of the validity of my position or of the mission's. I had said my lines as expected, and I was in.

I lived through the rest of those three days, wishing that they might somehow be shortened, for I wanted to return to my field and begin trying out in earnest the things which were being talked about at such length. The Work was the supreme subject and object of everyone present, it seemed to me, and human relationships went by the board. Except for Lynn, no one seemed to be an individual. They were cogs in wheels, fitting smoothly into their notches, emitting the right kind of squeak—and this, I thought, was as it should be if the task of each was the same. What room was there for questionings, or the exercise of individuality? In answer to an inquiry I had learned to which mission Lynn belonged, and I heard that she had been on the verge of resigning or being asked to resign—my informant was not certain which—but her unimpeachable record as a physician and a missionary kept her superiors from dealing too harshly.

Between the hymn singing and the praying and the

reporting and the devotionals there was time for "fellow-ship," which usually meant food eaten in the company of other missionaries and the sharing of a few jokes and personal anecdotes. I longed to have more conversation with Lynn—or, for that matter, with anyone who would take time seriously to discuss issues—but there was no opportunity. So I settled for faithful attendance at all meetings, where I tried to learn all I could.

CHAPTER

12

ON THE morning after my return home I was making coffee for breakfast, thinking of the victorious testimonies of the many missionary-conquerors at the conference. I, too, must fling out my banner with joy—it is God who will lead me in triumph. When I opened the canister in which I kept the coffee I noticed a slightly moldy smell instead of the rich aroma I had anticipated. I put the can closer to my nose. It was definitely moldy. I had no other coffee in the house. Should I throw this away? Certainly not. No missionary had a right to be fussy about such a trifle. I had left home and kindred to come here in obedience to Christ and would I balk at drinking a cup of ill-tasting coffee? I put the grounds in the pot and proceeded with the meal. It was a victory. A very small victory, to be sure, but nevertheless an indication of singlemindedness. People back in the States with their vacuum-packed Maxwell House—what did they know of doing without? "God, I thank Thee. . . ." The words of the Pharisee, "that I am not as other men" flashed through my mind, not as the words of the Pharisee but as my own, as the prayer of my heart. I was thankful that I was not like others who had ignored the call. Immediately upon the recognition that I had in sincerity said the very words Jesus had condemned the Pharisee for saying, I prayed the prayer of the other in the story, "God, be merciful to me, a sinner."

I put the coffeepot on the table and sat down. A little book of daily readings from the Bible lay on the table, and I opened it to the portion for that day. "If we confess our sins, He is faithful and just to forgive us our sins, and to cleanse us from all unrighteousness." I thanked God for those words. I was a sinful missionary, but then God had entrusted the missionary task to sinners, and if we didn't do it, who would? Too many had left their responsibility unfulfilled. Some had suffered, sacrificed, sailed through bloody seas in order to carry the Light to those in darkness, but not many. "O God, to us may grace be given to follow in their train." As I buttered a roll I thought of the "noble army, men and boys, the matron and the maid," and managed to put myself into the lineup somewhere. I hummed over the other stanzas—the one about meeting the tyrant's brandished steel, the lion's gory mane. How gladly would I do that for the sake of Christ!

I finished the roll, drank the last of the coffee (a deed of courage unlikely ever to be sung about), and began to wash the dishes, thinking over in my mind how to attack the job today. It had all seemed so obvious at the conference. Each missionary had his program—he knew what needed to be done where, and he had a method for doing it. I knew what needed to be done here in the mountains: these poor pagan Quichuas needed to be told about Jesus Christ, and there was one thing above all others that was needed in order to do this—the Bible, translated into their own language.

I decided I would go out again today, try to find Pedro, speak to him about the possibility of working for me as an informant in the language. He was a normally intelligent Indian, I judged—perhaps a little above average, since he had a tile roof on part of his house and enough initiative to work in the market place. I would offer him more than he could earn as a *cargador*, we would have regular sessions on the language, I would teach him the Bible bit by bit as we went along, and I would trust God to open his eyes to his own need of a Savior and then to the need of his own people. He would then be eager to help with the translation of the Scripture. When the Quichuas had the Bible and had been given the opportunity to learn to read it, the responsibility would rest with them to accept or reject the message I had brought.

As I finished the housework, this outline of my plan appeared to me as wholly feasible. Why had I made it all so complicated? I chose a few tracts to carry in my pocket, put on my coat and left the house, walking in the direction of the main plaza. The day was cold, with only thin sunlight filtering through a white sky. There was the feel of rain in the air. This would be a blessing, for the dust lay thick on the road and on the geraniums in my front yard. The rain would make it colder and even more bleak and desolate than it was ordinarily, but it would wash my flowers and clean my lungs. Days of cold, driving wind forced the gritty dust deep into my sinuses and lungs so that each breath seemed to scrape and scratch. How good a rain would be!

When I reached the plaza I was startled to find hordes of Indians converging toward it, far more than the usual market-day crowd, and yet there were fewer stalls set up. There was an atmosphere of jubilance and gaiety I had not seen before. Hats danced in the sunlight and I could hear music coming from somewhere—the birdlike notes of panpipes and the plinking of a guitar. A great throng was pouring from the cathedral on the other side of the market place. It must be a feast day. I went into the little grocery store where I did most of my food buying.

"*Buenos días*, señora," I said. "What is happening to-day?"

"*Buenos días*, señorita. Do you not know? This is the day of the fiesta."

"A fiesta? Of what?"

"Of the saint."

"Which saint?" I realized I should have known who the patron saint of the town was.

"Of our San Rafael, señorita. It is the biggest fiesta of the year."

How could I have been so ignorant? I could see the woman's incredulity. Ah, these foreigners. I made a few small purchases and went out to watch. Groups of Indians stood here and there, some of them sharing a bottle, some talking, others watching and waiting. The stalls were doing a brisk business selling food and drinks, but there were no clothing stalls open today and I noticed that many of the shops which bordered the plaza were locked and barred. Gradually I became aware of distant shouting and music. There was a movement among those in the plaza, and attention turned to the southwest corner. A crowd of Indians was moving toward the corner, as though preparing for some encounter. I could not make out what was happening. Suddenly a mob of shouting, flailing Indians rushed into the plaza and the crowd swirled and heaved, women and children backed out of the way, policemen swore and swung clubs, and I saw that six or eight free-for-all fights had broken out among the men. In no time it seemed that everyone in the plaza was fighting or cheering for the fighters. The woman from the store had come out of her shop and was standing beside me.

"Why are they fighting, señora?" I asked.

"Oh, it is not permitted any longer, but they used to fight for possession of the plaza."

"For possession of the plaza?"

"Yes, in order to be the leaders of the dance. It is the custom. Perhaps an ancient custom, but that is the way they are, the Indians. They have their customs." She shrugged.

"And now it is against the law?"

"So they say. But who can stop them? And then, the fiestas bring good business."

From another street which gave onto the plaza came a procession of Indians bearing huge candles garlanded with wax flowers and paper streamers. Umbrellas bobbed up and down in the midst of the throng and I heard a weird, melancholy chant. As they spread out into the square I could see that images were being carried under the umbrellas. People jostled for positions nearer to the images, and I caught a glimpse of the face of one old Indian woman, withered as a dried apricot, but with brilliant, intense eyes, joyously following the figure of the Virgin. There was in that look a great hope, the first hope I had seen in an Indian face. Those in the front ranks moved with a springiness in the step, turning their faces back toward the Blessed Mother and surging forward as though drawing the worshipers along with an invisible harness. The music, too, seemed to rise and fall in waves with the surging of the crowd.

In the center of the plaza a band began to play, drowning out the panpipes and guitars with a blast of tubas, trombones and trumpets. They were white men and mestizos who made up the band, and I gathered that they had been hired for the occasion, which was clearly an Indian celebration. White people stood in doorways around the square and watched from balconies and windows, but it was the Indians who today had possession of the town. They began to dance, chanting and stamping in circles, their ponchos swinging, bare feet pounding the earth. There were also men dressed in odd pieces of white men's clothing—sweaters, high-top boots, a policeman's hat or a pair of sunglasses adding a bizarre flourish to the shapeless calf-length trousers and homespun shirts of every day. I found something pitiable and touching about this attempt to assume the white man's status for a day. Inhibitions were forgotten as they gave themselves to the celebration, whirling and throwing back their heads, lifting their elbows and knees with a gay energy, bowing and strutting imperiously. The whole plaza was by now thronged with Indians, some of them fighting, some drinking at the booths, some dancing or playing instruments, some still standing in groups along the edges, some eager and adoring as they followed the processions to the cathedral. The images were being carried into the church to be blessed at the Mass which was soon to be said. Women squatted on the steps selling candles and garlands.

"This must be a very important Mass for them, isn't it?" I asked my friend.

"Yes, señorita. The fiesta Mass is the greatest of the year for this town."

"And they bring the images from their own villages to the Mass?"

"Yes, señorita, to be blessed. They bring them from far away, some of them, and then they take them back again to bless the village."

I wondered why the white people did not participate more in the festival. They were Catholics, the fiesta seemed to be a Catholic one, so why should the participants be only Indians? The custom must have its roots far back in Indian tradition.

The crowd pressed me back toward the walls of the shops and I saw that a new attraction was moving down the street. Several figures dressed in huge, elaborately decorated headdresses with grotesque masks were weaving crazily toward me, flanked by laughing, singing men, men playing tambourines and flutes and panpipes. The shape of the headdresses and the features on the masks reminded me startlingly of the Tibetan devil dancers I had once seen in a missionary film. The decorations were Oriental in character and coupled with the Mongolian features of the faces which surrounded them, reminded me of the mystery of the origin of these people. Where were they when the Apostle Paul wrote, "How shall they hear without a preacher? . . . But I say, Have they not heard? Yes verily, their sound went into all the earth, and their words unto the ends of the world." If Paul meant by "all the earth" all of the known world, where did the American Indian fit into God's design? How was it possible that they had heard the Gospel, and if they had not what provision had God made for the generations which had died before the era of Christian foreign missions? I had heard such questions discussed by people who were considered authorities on missionary work. The answers they gave were facile, and, to me, meaningless.

Here before me was a pageant of paganism, labeled, however, with Christian saints' names, which had its roots probably thousands of years ago, in a past civilization of which almost nothing was known. These Indians had been

[133]

subjugated by the Incas before the Spanish Conquest, but no one knew to which tribes they had belonged before that. The Incas had perhaps introduced a new significance to the ancient rites of the conquered tribes and in their sun worship had obscured the original meaning. Another religion had more recently supplanted that of the sun, but vestiges of an unknown variety of religions probably remained.

I stood for a long time, watching the dancing, listening to the strange, sad music—when the hired bands stopped their thumping and shrieking, the music the Indians themselves were making came through in thin, plaintive tones. The sour odors of gin and *chicha* became stronger, Indians kept pouring into the plaza until it seemed that there was not room for one more. They danced and sang and drank and went into the church and came out. Finally, some receded into the shops. Others who had bundles of blankets and food with them, and mothers who were carrying their babies, began to set up camp in doorways, under portals, on the sidewalk, wherever they could find a space.

"Will they stay the night?" I asked the señora.

"Oh, yes, señorita! They will stay several nights. You do not understand, señorita. This is a big occasion. Some will go home and come back, but they like to be together. This is their great pleasure, the fiesta. What else have they, the poor things?"

"Their lives are hard, aren't they?" I said.

"Well, yes. It is hard, the life of an Indian. But it does not matter to them. They are used to it."

Like animals. I remembered what the señora had said to me once about the Indians. She called them "poor things," condescendingly, as one might perhaps call a fool or a dumb beast poor. There was no compassion in her tone.

She said they did not mind a hard life. What did they know of any other kind? I yearned to help them. There was, obviously, nothing I could do for them here at the fiesta. I had come to find Pedro but he was nowhere to be seen, and if I did find him how could I intrude my request into his celebration? I was wholly outside the pale for the time being, and must content myself with talking to the shop-keeper.

Perhaps, on second thought, this was why I had come to the plaza today. Perhaps this would be my opportunity to win her. I could not help feeling that a contact with a white woman was second best, but it was clear to me now that this was a day set apart for Indians, and I as a white woman and a foreigner could have no part in it. Ancient loyalties, an irrepressible consciousness of their mystic heritage of a long-forgotten god or system, brought the Indians thronging to the fiesta, eager to give themselves up to the power of the mob, the images, the liquor. Their habitual sullenness and deference to the white man were flung to the winds. I watched them take over the white man's town, crowd out his shops, even elbow him roughly off the sidewalk. Police clumped around through the crowd, half-heartedly seeking to maintain some semblance of order.

The sky overhead had been rapidly darkening although the hour was close to noon, and rain clouds rolled in ominous heaps from the eastern cordillera. Wind blew the dust in tangled veils as the merrymakers scuffed it up with their bare feet. I did not want to be caught in a downpour but was held fascinated by the sights before me. All at once there was a crash from almost directly behind me, several shouts, and the door of a little eating place was flung outward with a bang. A group of Indians erupted, tearing and beating at one another, and I saw in the center of the group a man, half carried and half dragged, whose nose was bleeding profusely.

"Ay, what barbarity!" said the señora, who had been attending a customer in her shop and had come out again when she heard the fracas. "Leave him! Leave him!" The Indians paid no attention, one or two of them still flailing at the others, and the man with the bleeding nose stumbled to his feet and faded into the crowd. The señora went back into her shop.

"Those savages. There is nothing one can do with them when they are drunk. They are savages, animals. They ought to be shut up in prison, but then there is no way to do that. All of them would be in prison. What is there to do? *Caramba!*"

Rain began to fall in huge drops, hitting the dust with little soft explosions, sending up a wet earthy smell, but the dancing went on. Some of the men who had folded the edges of their ponchos up onto their shoulders unfolded them, a few went to push their blankets and bundles closer together against the walls, but most of them seemed oblivious of the weather, of the time of day or the presence of any but their own people. Their stiff felt hats acted as umbrellas and they laughed and chanted and marched and drank and fought and allowed themselves to be what they could never be on an ordinary day. They knew, today, who they were; they accepted themselves and had the courage to reject the rest of us. Today they were able to believe, for a few shining moments, that the white man was not master of all that was good.

The rain was falling now in great gray rods, beating down on the plaza, splashing the water up against us as we stood under the narrow overhang in front of the shops, and I decided it was time to go home.

[136]

"When will the fiesta stop, señora?" I asked.

"*Caramba*, señorita, it hasn't started yet!"

"If I come back later this afternoon will they still be dancing?"

"Of course! And tomorrrow and the next day." She spread her palms open in front of her shoulders in the Latin gesture of futility. "Drinking and dancing, dancing and drinking—nothing but death will stop them, señorita!"

"Well, then, I think I will go home for a little while. But I do want to see the fiesta. I would like to know all about the life of the Indians."

"When you have seen the fiesta, you will know all. What else is there? What more do they do?" Again she shrugged and lifted her palms.

"Who knows?" I said. "Well, señora, until later. I am going now."

"Until later, señorita."

The rain was pelting down, but I hurried through it toward my house, ruining my shoes but eager for the peace and silence I would find at home.

The dust was washed from the geraniums and from the tiles of my roof, making the reds and oranges clean and bright once more. Water raced between the stones of my front walk, pouring in deltas of mud into the street, streaming in sheets from the eaves. A cold stream ran down my neck as I unlocked the door, but once inside I could not hear the tumult. The rain made a soft murmur which mingled with the ticking of my little Swiss clock. I liked the little clock. It had a pale green enamel case with delicately painted birds, and the hands were lacy. Inside was a charming music box which played the Kaiser waltz. It was really the only thing I had which was personal and permanent in the house, and its gentle sound spoke to me

[137]

like a familiar voice. It was better to be alone, with this small voice and this innocuous face, than to be in a crowd where, because I did not belong, I was even more alone. The faces and the voices in the plaza were directed to something from which I was excluded. Would I ever succeed in being included by the Indians? But the thought of being included in so strange a celebration frightened me, for it was not a thing of which I could or wished to be a part. No, it was not mere inclusion I sought. I wanted them only to open the door a crack so that I could get a foot in. I did not want to be taken into the house. I wanted to take them out of it. And I would have to lure or trick them into coming out.

The impossibilities mounted before me. To try to know the Indians—who had done this before? To be accepted by them—what white man, let alone white woman, had achieved this? To live beside them, as though one of them, but with designs. This idea began to disturb me. The private designs, the double-heartedness which were inescapable made me feel like a conspirator, and although I imagined that some might find excitement in being a part of a plot, I myself could not be set at ease.

As I put the things I had bought into the cupboards in the kitchen, I remembered that I had not seen Pedro, who had been the object of my visit to the plaza. Poor Pedro. He had not the faintest idea that he was a part, too, in a plot—he thought that for once he had met a guileless white person.

The fiesta lasted for three days, and for part of each day I went and stood by the shop and watched. Mercedes, the señora's little daughter, took me around the corner to watch a special dance in a private courtyard. The cacophony of conflicting bands in the plaza would have prevented my hearing the music in the courtyard, and I wondered how many other patios held such groups. About a dozen Indians were reeling and prancing to the boom of a bass drum and the creak of three or four cornets. I stood at the arched entrance with Mercedes, unnoticed by most of the crowd, and listened carefully to the music to see if I could follow any tune. It was very jerky, with sudden plunges and shrieks in addition, it seemed, to the unplanned ones due to the musicians' lack of skill. What was it that made it sound so different from music to which I was accustomed? I did not know very much about music, but had heard that the octave was not the only scale in the world's music, and perhaps this music used a different scale. Was it the pentatonic? I listened some more, and could single out no more than five notes. Yes, that must be what gave it the jerky quality, the wide gaps between notes.

"What is this dance, Mercedes?" I asked the child.

"It is a dance, señorita. They are dancing."

"Yes, I see. But does the dance mean something special?"

"It is a dance of the fiesta."

"But—why would it be that they dance back here in this patio, away from the others in the plaza?"

"Who knows why it will be? They dance for the fiesta of San Rafael, señorita."

I could learn nothing further, though it seemed a very earnest, exclusive group, bent on performing to their utmost whatever it was they were dedicated to doing.

We visited a few of the cafés. Mercedes did not really understand my interest in all of this. Who wanted to watch Indians drink and fight? But she took me. She also guided me through the cathedral, where tawdry jewelry decked hideous plaster images, five-sucre bills covered another, candles flickered and dripped in front of various figures of the Virgin, a priest was intoning something in a little chapel to one side, and black-veiled women knelt to pray. Indians were genuflecting here and there, clasping their hands and moving their lips.

On the last day the plaza was littered with drunken Indians, and little groups dragged one and then another, trying to get them out of the way of the traffic, pleading and cajoling with them to get up and come home. Wives heaved and dragged their besotted husbands, two drunken men wove violently back and forth trying to support each other, heads lolling and eyes rolling. Little children sat and cried in the gutters beside stupefied mothers and fathers. I watched them gradually vacate the plaza, winding up the streets toward their mountainsides. Perhaps if I followed up the street a little way I could help someone. I started in the direction of my own house, seeing several families passing that way. A woman with a baby on her back was stumbling along, clearly on the verge of slumping into the gutter. Her husband, shouting something unintelligible to the skies, grabbed her arm, shoved her, and she fell in a heap, miraculously keeping the baby upright in his sling on her back. He began to wail and she flung her shoulder back as though trying to dislodge him; he screamed louder and she fell forward and lay still. Her husband bent over her in bewilderment as though searching for something and then fell heavily on top of her. I quickened my pace, seeing that this had started a fight. The woman was yelling, thrusting wildly at the man with her fist. He had hold of her hair and was twisting the braid, slapping her face with the other hand. I feared not only for the woman but for the baby on her back.

"Leave her alone!" I cried. "What is going on?"

Both stopped immediately and looked around, their eyes shifting uncertainly into focus. I saw that it was Pedro and Rosa, but they did not recognize me. They gave me a look that said, "Mind your own business," and set at one another again. I tried then to interfere by pulling Pedro's arm. He turned on me with a curse. His lip was swollen with a cut or bruise of some kind, his hair was matted over his forehead and his eyes were bloodshot. At that moment he recognized me, and it was as though blinds were drawn over his face. The intensity of his anger and the freedom of his drunkenness, the real person beneath the humble exterior I had known up until now, receded at once and he looked at me darkly, resentfully.

"Can I help you, Pedro? Rosa?" I hesitated, not knowing what to say.

"*Buenas tardes*, señorita," said Pedro. Even his state of stupor, his anger, and his resentment at my intrusion did not prevent the automatic courtesy.

"*Buenas tardes*, Pedro." Again I had forgotten to greet him. "Can I help you? Are you going home?"

"Home, señorita. *Buenas tardes*, señorita. We are going home."

"May I come with you?" I thought surely they would never reach their destination alone, and I pitied the baby, wriggling and crying on Rosa's back.

"To the house, señorita. Yes. *Buenas tardes*. We are going home, señorita. Until another day, señorita," said Pedro. Probably he was too drunk to have understood my offer, so I tried again. "Can I help you? Can I go home with you?"

"Until another day, señorita. We are going." He was struggling desperately to get to his feet, and I gathered that this was no time to impose help where it was not wanted.

He yanked Rosa to her feet and the pair zigzagged up the road and around the corner of a mud wall, the baby bobbing crazily and watching me from under the brim of his felt hat. It was that look again—the same look I'd seen in Guayaquil. The baby was contented and secure. His parents had him, they had their rare pleasures, they had each other. They were not going to call on me for help of any kind, drunk or sober, and it was I who would have to pursue their help. I stood in the middle of the road and stared at the mud wall behind which they had disappeared.

THERE WAS one drugstore in Indi Urcu, and it was the shop
I most liked to visit. It was small, but wonderfully neat,
with a very high ceiling and rows and rows of bottles and
boxes, many of which had familiar brand names of imported preparations. The smell of the place was antiseptic
and fresh, a welcome change from the hot grease and garlic
odors of the stuffy shops. The little man who ran the
drugstore was as neat as his shop; he wore a white coat
with a comb sticking out of the breast pocket and his hair
was always impeccably slicked. He treated me with great
deference, always searching out the American product
when a European or Ecuadorian one would have served.
He never called me *madamita*—it was "Ah! La señorita!
Buenos días, señorita!" whenever I came in, and I had the
feeling that he understood my position in the town—he
knew it was difficult, he knew I wanted to help people, and
he was one with me in the desire, for he wanted very much
to help me.

I stopped in one morning on my way to the post office
and as I finished making my small purchase an Indian with
a deep gash in his head came in asking for a remedy. When
he confessed that he had no money the little druggist rolled

his eyes toward the ceiling and lifted his palms with a shrug.

"*No hay que hacer.*" Nothing can be done.

The Indian pressed a rag to his neck, where blood was staining his collar, looked helplessly from the druggist to me and started toward the door.

"Can I help you?" I asked.

"I have no money," he said.

"That is not important," I told him. "Let me buy you something."

He eyed me dubiously, while the druggist watched me with mild amusement.

"What happened?" I said.

"I was working on a house. A big beam fell on my head."

"Where is the boss?"

"He told me not to work any more."

"Did he say he would pay for your medicine?" As soon as I asked the question I saw from the faces of both men how naïve it was.

"He said Go, señorita. The boss said Go."

"But he paid you for your work?"

"Not today, señorita. He just said Go."

I bought some Mercurochrome and adhesive tape and did the best I could to make a bridge over the wound. It was hard to make the tape stick to the bloodied hair, and it was equally hard to make him believe that he did not owe me any money. The druggist took my payment without a word while the Indian stood, hat in hand, by the door, still wondering what was expected of him. I wanted very much to ask his name, but feared he would think I intended to track him down for payment, so I merely said, "Until another day," and he answered, "May God pay you," and followed me out.

Oh, this town, this white man's town! Even my little drugstore and my nice little man. But I had met another Indian, as it were by chance. Surely God had ordained the meeting, for He was with me.

The sun shone as it nearly always did in the mornings, and the market place was buzzing. I saw here and there friends I had made, greeted them, happy to find them in their accustomed stalls, and then my steps quickened toward the post office. It was a never-fading delight to go there, past the stamp kiosks, past the little boy who sold magazines on the steps, into the dark little rotunda walled with boxes, each with its tiny window and brass keyhole. "As cold waters to a thirsty soul, so is good news from a far country." That was it. Today there was just one letter. It had an Ecuadorian stamp. Woodrow Rogers in Guayaquil. I tore it open.

"You will be sorry to learn that the Gardners have finally been rejected by the mission on medical grounds. We know how you have looked forward to their coming to work with you, to establish the school. The board feels that if you would prefer to be transferred to a station with another couple on it this might be worked out, although we would be reluctant to see Indi Urcu without a worker. . . .

"God's ways are not our ways. This is of course a great disappointment to all of us, but we must accept it from Him."

Indi Urcu without a worker. No, I could not consider that. I knew that the place in the vineyard to which God had most certainly brought me was His place for me to stay, and although, by worldly standards, it was not an enviable position, it was the object of my most cherished ambitions, a corner of the earth in which to serve my Master, a people to call my people. Would I be willing to

[145]

labor on alone? The idea of being a solitary missionary was not unthinkable to me—after all, if I had faced the possibility of never marrying (and what calling could more effectively reduce one's chances, if the statistics I had seen were correct? Sixteen women to one man!)—if I was willing to be single, I should be willing to work alone. This kind of hardship fitted in with what I had half expected. But some kind of revision in my outlook was called for. How was I to accept a negative answer to so many people's prayers? The Gardners had been thoroughly prayed for. They had gone so far as to sell their home, they had booked a passage, they had bought their outfit. They had their financial support pledged by several churches, and at the last minute they were stopped by what seemed a very minor physical disability. Could not God have seen to that? It was not mere companionship for a single woman that was at stake. It was not simply the plans of a mission board or a family that had gone awry. The needs of a whole section of Indian population would be unmet. Even if another couple were found to take their place, what of the scores who daily passed into eternity during the delay? I could agree that God's ways are not our ways, all right. But why did we insist on trying to make them so? Was it possible, after all, that the reasons for the shortage of missionaries were sometimes inscrutable, not to be explained so simply as "The church of God is asleep"?

I walked slowly out of the post office, wondering where to turn. The market with its pushing women and their baskets, its jostling men and beasts, its reeking stalls, ordinarily a merely bustling place, seemed to me now in a frenzy of business. If I could just sort them out, shut them up, carry them off to some quiet place, apart, where I could sit them down and say to them, *Listen. God wants to speak to you.* But no. That was of course out of the question, and I could only clench the letter in my hand and send up a desperate prayer, Lord God, *how* will You get through to them?

I worked my way along the sidewalk. My part, the translation of the Scriptures, ought to go hand in hand with other aggressive efforts to help the people. Education was the obvious wedge, and the Gardners were supposed to do that. Now what would happen? Nobody to start a school, no bait to catch the Indians.

There was a sign over a door that I passed, *"Se pone inyecciones,"* and lettered faintly on the door itself was the word *"Clínica."* I had assumed when I first saw that sign that it meant the presence of a doctor, but had learned that there was no doctor nearer than Wairapamba. A woman who did not even qualify as a nurse had been authorized to give injections, and this was the extent of medical service in the village. Perhaps it was medicine that would provide the wedge if education would not. The idea took hold at once—not that I had had any training, but there might be a lot I could do with common sense and compassion, and was it mere coincidence that I had treated the wounded Indian, received the letter, and noticed again that sign, all within an hour?

I began carrying along a small bag of medicines on my visits to the Indians—aspirin, worm medicine, DDT powder for the ubiquitous head lice, a few first-aid things. Nearly always there were minor needs which I could meet, but often the Indians wanted to know why I did not have a needle to stick them with. "A needle, señorita, is good for anything. Why do you not have a needle?" I explained that I was not a doctor, but this was hardly an explanation to them.

[147]

There was a pregnant girl in the house up beyond Rosa's—I had talked to her several times, a girl not more than seventeen, with an unusually Oriental look about her, smooth, high cheekbones and almond-shaped eyes, and she wore delicate gold earrings in her pierced ears. I would hardly have guessed she was pregnant, for she carried herself beautifully and wore full skirts, but Rosa mentioned it casually one day and I thought how exciting it would be if the girl would let me help in her delivery. It took some nerve on my part to suggest this to her, for I had never done more than watch two births, when a nurse friend of mine, before I came to Ecuador, had secured permission for me to do this in a hospital. I had read one book on midwifery which said that clean hands and common sense were the two basic requirements, and I was confident that I could meet those at least, which was probably more than the old Indian women who were called in to help could have done. Their brand of "common sense," I feared, was often nothing more than superstition. The girl nodded noncommittally at my proposal.

"You send someone to call me when the pain starts," I said.

"*Arí*," she said.

"I would like very much to come and help you," I said.

"*Arí*."

A few weeks later Rosa told me the girl had died in childbirth. Why hadn't they called me? How had she died? Rosa did not know. Was the child living? Oh no, it, too, had died.

"How sad," I said.

"Oh well, señorita, it was a wind child."

"A wind child?"

"That's what it was."

[148]

"And what is a wind child?"

"A child born of the wind. It had no other father." And Rosa rubbed her grindstone over the corn.

"But the poor girl. Perhaps if they had called me I could have saved her."

"Perhaps so, perhaps not." Back and forth went the stone. Rosa was right. Perhaps not. And what sort of beginning would that have made?

I kept on the watch for opportunities I might dare to use. I did not want really serious cases if I could avoid them, for I knew how dangerous my little knowledge might be. But I found an item in the newspaper one day about a case of smallpox which had been discovered in a town about twenty miles from Indi Urcu. The government had been vaccinating school children wherever there was a local doctor who could carry out the program. I found from the principal of the Indi Urcu school that he would be only too glad to allow the children to be vaccinated if I could find a doctor who would come. Lynn Anderson had traveled much in the mountains, holding clinics and cooperating with local authorities in medical work, and I wrote to my mission board asking if I might invite her to come and spend a few days with me, vaccinating the children and visiting Indian homes. It might be possible, I added, to announce a clinic to be held in my home during that time, and this could prove an opening wedge in the town as well as in the Indian community.

Lynn's schedule was full, but she arranged to come. I spent hours going from one Indian house to another, inviting them to come to the clinic. I was mystified one afternoon to see a bus stop at my gate—one of those great, swollen wooden things with no aisle down the center into which Indians packed themselves for interminable, airless journeys through the thin atmosphere of the high altitude. What on earth was it doing stopping at my gate? Lynn got off. A small boy swung her sleek blue suitcase off the top of a pile of burlap sacks on the roof of the bus and she came in, looking unrumpled and chic in a gray wool suit with a dark red silk scarf tying her hair back.

"Lynn! Why, I never dreamed you'd have to come in one of those things! Oh dear, the journey must have been awful! I sort of thought maybe Mr. MacDonald . . ."

"Why, it was nothing at all. We had a lovely ride, and the driver was so kind as to bring me up here after he'd let off the other passengers in the plaza."

Dear Lynn! How wonderful of her to come. How exciting it would be to show her around the town, to take her to see my Indians.

There were forty-six children in the school, and seven of these were Indians, the sons of "free Indians," the school-teacher told me. When I asked what this meant, he explained that many of the Indians in the area were the property of white landowners and did not own their land or their homes. Those who had sent their sons to school had learned through hard experience in the market that white men had a strong advantage over them because they could read and do fast arithmetic. So they had sent their children to school, even though it was very expensive for the children to board in town and it was out of the question for them to walk from their own homes daily.

When the teacher, a young white man in his late twenties, lined up the children for their vaccinations, the seven Indian children were at the end of the line. When they sat down again, I noticed that their seats were at the rear of the room and instead of individual desks like the others' they had a table between them.

The procedure was very simple. I swabbed the arm with alcohol, Lynn scratched it with a needle and applied the vaccine. The teacher maintained the strictest discipline, ordering his pupils around with short, sharp commands. His commands to the Indian children, it seemed to me, were shorter yet, and considerably sharper. One small boy had a hard time rolling his sleeve up high enough to suit Lynn.

"Hurry up! *Caramba!*" said the teacher and cuffed the back of the child's head.

The teacher had given no explanation to the children of the need for vaccine. They submitted willingly to the treatment, though fear showed in some of their faces. Little knowledge did they have of the disease from which they were being protected, much less any desire to be saved from it. If only missionary work were so simple, I reflected. If people could be corralled and injected, like so many cattle branded, without explanation or persuasion or personal sense of need. I had heard missionaries say, "I gave him the Gospel!" as though it had been an injection, and now, as the comparison presented itself, I began to ponder just how important it might be that an individual be prepared for the Gospel. Lynn talked quietly to the children as she vaccinated, and I could feel the tension ease. They even seemed sorry when it was time for us to go, for they saw that she was their friend.

As we left the building, it was gratifying to think of it as a little island of safety, where forty-six human beings were now beyond the reach of a serious disease, simply because Lynn and I had come and spent an hour there.

We walked back up the street toward my house and saw the valley spread out before us, an endless stretch of tiny square fields and little thimble houses sheltering hundreds and thousands of people who were in jeopardy from the same disease, and did not know it. What of them? I spoke of this to Lynn.

She had a way of not responding immediately, of walking on as though she had not heard, and this time, when she was silent, I thought what a bromide my question must have seemed to her. Her reply, however, simple and direct, registered no scorn: "Yes. I suppose anyone who tries to help people in any way soon becomes overwhelmed with the endlessness of the task. So he has two choices. He can give up at the start, or he can accept his limitations and go on doing what he can."

Accept his limitations. This was an idea I had not thought very much about. I was serving the God of the Impossible. Words like "vision" and "challenge" flashed like illuminated captions over my picture of missionary life, and, as I walked along the road with Lynn and my eyes swept the vast bowl of the valley, they still seemed appropriate captions. But when we turned in at my front gate and found the yard filled with people who had heard by the village grapevine of the presence of the *doctora americana* the words blinked out again. Here before us was a definable task, a smaller sacrifice, a commoner duty. The people were mostly of the *mestizo* or *cholo* class—of mixed Indian and white blood, the women with long braids and plaid shawls and shoes and stockings, the men in blue jackets and rope sandals or shoes.

They were silent as we came into the yard, but when we opened the door they pressed around us, trying to get first place.

"I have been here many hours, *doctora*, and I am very sick."

"My daughter here, please, *doctora*, she is very grave."

"Do me the favor, señorita *doctora*, of attending to me, for the love of God!"

Lynn smiled kindly at them and explained that we were not yet ready to see patients, but that she would do her best to see them all in turn. I looked eagerly to see if there were any Indians in the crowd. Their needs were so great, and they had so little means for meeting them. They seldom had money to buy even drugstore medicines, and would not dream of going to Wairapamba to consult a doctor. Why had they not come? The Indians knew the doctor was coming, but there was not a single Indian in the group.

As I set water on the stove to boil and began spreading sheets on the table and laying out bandages and medicines according to Lynn's instructions, I tried to see how it was all to work. I had come to Indi Urcu to minister to Indians, and the means introduced for reaching them succeeded only in bringing to my door white people, those to whom not only did I feel no call, but whose presence inhibited the Indians' coming. It was ironic and I could work up little enthusiasm for the work ahead of us this afternoon. At least it would be good experience, for I could watch Lynn and learn from her and perhaps God would let me use the knowledge gained to help Indians in the future. If I were going to settle for the possible, which I had almost disdained, it was only in the hope that ultimately the impossible would be attained. The *cholos* came at the first invitation (which had not really been meant for them), to offer their aches and pains to the doctor and to take from her whatever she chose to give. The Indians, whose aches and pains were far deeper and less curable, did not come. They had received the invitation, but they did not come. They had not learned to ask anything of the white man. They had learned, instead, to bear their own burdens and this they did, day after day, year in and year out, in the loneliness of the high Andes, in the cold of their fireless huts, on the windswept plains of the grass country where their sheep grazed, and in the hostile white man's village where they knew they were despised. It was their life, and they did not dream that it could be changed.

We took the patients one by one into the living room and Lynn listened to their complaints, many of which seemed to have to do with the liver or kidneys. They were mostly women, and they screwed up their faces with pain and doubled over, a hand kneading the ailing area as they described the attacks. There were one or two cases of advanced tuberculosis, a man with a hernia which had been operated on in a hospital in Riobamba, but they had sewed his insides into knots, Lynn said, and nothing would help him but another operation. There was a young girl, her face gray with pain, who had what she called an earache that hurt her whole head. Mastoid, Lynn said, and nothing could be done for her unless she would go to a hospital. The girl turned in silence to her hovering young husband.

"Is it very serious, *doctora?*" he asked.

"Yes, it is serious. She must go to a hospital."

"Can't you cure her here?"

"No, I can do nothing for her here except give her a pill for the pain. But her ear will only get worse."

"Will they want to operate in the hospital? Will they cut?"

"They will have to operate."

The man stood silent for a moment, fear growing in his eyes. "Is there no other remedy?"

"No. I am very sorry."

The girl shifted the baby in her shawl, her great dark eyes moving from Lynn to her husband and back again.

[154]

The man murmured a syllable to her and they went out. Hospital was out of the question for them. Who would pay? The despair in their faces found no answer.

There was no time for lunch. Throughout the afternoon they came, for word spreads rapidly in the sierra in spite of great distances. The foreign doctor was there, and was not charging anything for consultations. She tried to collect a nominal fee for the medicines she dispensed but that was all. A few gave promise of a chicken or a sack of potatoes when they came again.

I learned to give an injection and took notes as fast as I could on the questions Lynn asked and the treatments she gave. A sketchy way to learn medicine but far better than nothing, I told myself, and it was likely that the same maladies would recur in this area.

There were various cases of malnutrition—strange bone formations, goiters, rashes and skin eruptions, anemia. Lynn prescribed vitamins and iron pills, fruits and vegetables, but the people nodded so enthusiastically that we could not help feeling they had no intention of following any consistent course of treatment. They were willing to swallow a pill or two today, but they would see no need for it tomorrow, especially if the pain was lessened at all. As for eating fruits and vegetables, how absurd. They had come to the doctor for medicine, not for food. They themselves knew what to eat.

At the end of the day, as the sun began to drop behind the mountains, I looked out to see how many patients remained. I was astonished to find Pedro just coming in the gate.

"*Buenas tardes*, Pedro," I said.

" '*S tardes*, señorita. Is the *doctora* here?"

"Yes. You have come to see her?"

"Yes."

He came in silently and began to roll up his trouser leg until we could see a deep, festering wound in the muscle of his calf.

"How did you do that?" asked Lynn.

"It is cut, *doctora*."

"With a knife, no?"

"It hurts me very much."

"How long have you had it?"

"A long time."

Lynn knew there would be no more information forth-coming and set about cleansing and bandaging the wound. Then she administered an injection of penicillin and instructed Pedro to come back for three days in a row so that I could put the needle into him again. She went over again with me the procedure for the injection, and wrote down the dosage.

"*Sí*, señorita," said Pedro.

"Three more days, Pedro. Tomorrow, and the day after that, and the day after that."

"*Sí*, señorita."

"You will not forget?"

He smiled faintly. "Why would I forget?"

"You must be exhausted," I said to Lynn when we finally sat down to supper. "How many did we have?"

"I didn't keep count," she said.

"I should think there were sixty or seventy at least," I said.

"I suppose so. A beginning anyway. If only we could get them to follow up the treatment. That is what is so disheartening about village clinics—some of the cases are beyond help outside a hospital, most of them require a simple but regularly continued treatment—and this, too, is hopeless unless you can follow it up yourself. The people just don't see the need for it."

"You must see some spectacular cures now and then, don't you?—cases which make you feel it's worthwhile?"

"Yes," she said, and the pause this time was longer than usual. "I see some spectacular things all right. But I no longer look for things to make it, as you say, worthwhile."

"What do you mean?"

"I'm not sure I can make you understand what I mean." She stirred her tea and laid the silver spoon carefully in the saucer and then raised her eyes, which were gray and widely spaced. The tiny lines around them, the weariness, did not cloud their kindness.

"You see, when I decided to be a doctor, it was because I wanted to help people. I thought, of course, that I *could* help people by being a doctor. So I went through seven years of study, and I came to Ecuador anticipating the good I was going to do. Gradually I came to see that the results which can be called good are few. And they cannot be the criterion for whether or not what we do is worthwhile. It is hopeless to try to weigh up the good, the bad, the futile, and the merely harmless, and hope that there will be enough of the good—in medical work, enough un-equivocal cures—to justify all the rest. Do you follow me?"

"I don't know. I think so. I mean, if the good doesn't justify the rest—is that what you said?" Lynn nodded. "Then what does?"

"Jesus told us to do what is true. I think the truth needs no justification, no defense."

PEDRO RETURNED for his shots as he had promised, and I took this as a happy omen. When the course of treatment was finished as Lynn had prescribed, the leg seemed much improved, but there was still a small opening which drained slightly, and I suggested to Pedro that it would be much better if he did not return to his work in the market place.

"But, señorita, I have to work. There is no money, and my land is very little."

"There are other ways to work, Pedro," I said.

"Not for me. I am a poor man. There is no other work."

"Pedro," I said. "would you like to work for me?"

"For you?" he asked in surprise. "What work? What can I do?"

"I would give you a job at which you could sit down."

"What, señorita? What do you mean, sit down?"

"Not only sit down, Pedro, but sit down in your own house!"

At this he laughed. "You want me to weave. Well, I am a good weaver, but I couldn't earn enough money that way. I earn more money carrying loads."

"No, Pedro. I don't want you to weave for me. I want you to teach me to speak your language."

"You will pay me for that?"

"Yes, Pedro, I will pay you for that. If you will let me come to your house every week—perhaps two or three times each week—and tell me stories in your own language —*your* language, Pedro, not Spanish—I will pay you. We will sit and talk, and then, someday, when I learn to speak, you will help me to translate God's word. I would pay you for that, too."

"You want so much to speak my language that you say, 'I will pay'?" Pedro was still not sure he had correctly understood me.

"Yes, Pedro, I say I will pay."

The idea finally sank in, we agreed on a price, and we began to spend several hours a day three times a week on my lessons. In that time Pedro earned what he would have made in the market in a five- or six-day week, and he seemed pleased with the plan. Rosa was harder to convince, and kept asking Pedro when he was going to town. When he showed her the money she wanted to know what I had given it to him for.

On the days when I was to go to Pedro's I tried to make my route different each time, and visit the huts I passed on the way. I had learned the elementary questions from Pedro and written them down on small cards which I carried in my pocket: "How are you?" "I am fine, and you?" "What is your name?" "Where do you live?" I practiced on a new and unsuspecting audience whenever I found one. Their initial astonishment usually gave place quickly to the urge to talk, and, having said as much as a sentence in Quichua, I found it hard to convince my listener that he had just heard the extent of my Quichua vocabulary. Fortunately this state of affairs did not continue for many days, and I was pleasantly surprised at the ease with which

I learned to give and take in conversation with an Indian who was willing to make even a slight effort to slow down for me.

When I got to Pedro's house we would sit down together by the fire sometimes, or, as I preferred, outdoors where the air was fresher and the light better. I liked the sunshine, in spite of cold wind and dust, but I think Pedro liked better the smell of smoke indoors and the snuffling of the guinea pigs. He loved to smoke as we talked, and very slowly and deliberately would roll his cigarettes, using any scrap of paper he had managed to find. He looked longingly at my small notebooks, the pages of which were exactly the size he needed, and I occasionally gave him a leaf although I knew he could not well afford to buy tobacco and I was not eager to encourage an expensive habit.

When I asked him about his grandparents, his crops or his children, he would sit for a long time, his knees pulled up under his poncho, his eyes fixed on the far mountains. He would blow a long blue curl of smoke, trying to think of the answer.

"My old fathers? The ones-who-lived-in-the-beginning? This whole valley, señorita—you see this valley?—this valley was filled with them, as many as the hair of your head." He gave the lock which hung in front of his ear a shake. "Very, very many they were, and they lived very well. All the land was theirs, the corn and the potatoes and barley, all the towns and all the houses, *all* was theirs, all belonged to the old fathers. Then, after that, the white man coming fooled them. The white man said he was a friend and the old fathers thought, We will live well with these people, but they were deceived. We do not remember that time. My father did not remember that time. It was long ago, señorita, in the beginning time. My grandfather did not remember it, but he had heard about it, and he used to tell me and my brothers about the beginning time. But when I was the size of Romero my grandfather was walking home from the village one afternoon—the sun was just about there"—Pedro stretched his arm toward the western sky, indicating by the angle how near the sun was to setting—"and high in the mountains it began to rain. It was not raining here, but we could see the black clouds and hear the thunder up the ravine. My grandfather was in the *quebrada*—you know the big *quebrada* up by Lame Pedro's house?—he was in there, coming home—he lived up there—and suddenly, suddenly the rain came, the water poured down like an avalanche through the *quebrada* and my grandfather died in the water. We found him the next morning at the bottom of the valley, down where the eucalyptus grows."

I was disappointed in Pedro's ignorance of the history of the Incas. He had no sense of heritage beyond the knowledge that his ancestors had once been free, and the owners of the land. Talk always turned to things he knew first- or second-hand. I asked him about his children, trying to find out if he had any idea of their ages.

"Romero was born the year the corn crop failed. I always sleep in my cornfield when it is ripe, but that year I slept in it for two months. No one had good corn, everyone wanted to steal. They would steal new corn, old corn, unripe corn. I hoped to save my corn, but in the end it was not worth the trouble. Let them steal it all, I said, take it, take it. And I went home from my field before the cock crowed and found that my wife had caused a child to be born, a man. But it was very small and thin and my wife said, 'What will we eat? We will die anyway, this child

[161]

will die, it is not worth raising, I will throw it away.' So she went outside—still the cock had not crowed—and threw the child away, just outside the wall. But my brother came along and found the child and picked it up and brought it back to my wife and said, 'Here, you must take care of this child, it is your child, is it not?' And she said 'It is my child,' and gave it the breast, and it grew. That is Romero. A good child, after all."

Pedro was intelligent enough to translate word for word when I asked for verb paradigms, and this was a great help in learning conjugations. It often happened, of course, that I asked him for a word which did not exist in Quichua, and he would then explain carefully in Spanish what the Spanish word I asked meant. He did not like to say that there was no Quichua equivalent. I could not resist asking *why* certain things were said in Quichua, why a suffix occurred here or an enclitic there, but soon came to understand that it was a useless question. What did I know of the *whys* of English? Why, for example, when it was correct to say "He went" was it not correct to say "Went he?" instead of "Did he go?" Suppose Pedro had asked me the meaning of *get?* I thought of the possibilities: get your coat, get married, get up, get in, get off, get caught, get out, this language gets me, get him to go, get away, get dinner, get lost. I was thankful I was not teaching English to Pedro.

Many hours were spent listening to stories the "old fathers" used to tell. Now that I had learned to follow the gist of a conversation or story I wanted to concentrate on specific forms of the language, and I taught Pedro to slow down and repeat. It took a great deal of effort to make him understand that by repeating I meant the very words he had spoken, rather than an interpretation or explanation. Finally he learned, and with the great patience characteristic of his people was eventually almost dictating legends and folk tales to me so that I could write every word in my notebooks and then study them at home, filing suffixes, words, syntax and sounds, memorizing phrases and analyzing forms. The content of the tales was just as fascinating to me, many of them dealing with the origins of things, the sun and stars, the seasons and animals, the winds and mountains and rocks. He told me of the legendary twins who, before they were born, guided their mother with instructions from the womb, and after their birth performed marvelous feats of magic and daring. Eventually the twins ascended into the heavens and became the morning and evening stars. There was the story of the condor who, like all other animals, had been a human being. His betrothed was the most beautiful virgin on earth, coveted by every man who saw her. The Sun God, too, saw her and wanted her for himself, so he took her off into the sky and the forsaken young man searched the earth until he became old and white-headed. Walking over the mountains in his black poncho, stooping to search every cranny for the beautiful girl, he finally was transformed into the huge bird which still hangs in the sky, his head bent toward the earth, his poncho outspread. "That is why he seizes our lambs, thinking to himself, 'Here is my woman.' "

The afternoons often found me trekking across the hills again, stopping in the fields to talk with Indians as they rested from plowing or hoeing, calling at huts where I found women weaving or nursing their babies. I was happy in these days, confident that the language work was basic and would one day bear fruit which would remain; gratified, too, to be living simply in a small village, moving about among the farm people as Jesus must have done. The things he talked about—sowing seed and plowing, seasons and harvests, sheep and cattle, lilies of the fields, birds of the air—all these things had their place in the lives of my Indians, and it seemed to me that Jesus Himself at times drew near and walked with me. At such moments I was transported by the vision of the great work which had been put into my hands to do. I saw the valley, filled with godless Quichuas, as my parish, and the open Bible, written at last in the language they could understand, as my gift to them.

The little smoky huts with their fleas and stench and darkness, which had at first repelled me and later aroused in me a great pity, I now accepted, as homes, the homes of people I knew. They took on a different aspect entirely, became a part of the furniture of my life, no longer forts of hostility. Inside their blackened walls I learned to respect the people who had built them—how admirably they had adapted themselves to so hostile an environment! Thatch was the only available roofing material, and it belonged to the landscape, to the great stretches of brown grass that glowed and breathed in the wind. The huts had no windows, not because the Indian loved darkness rather than light (though I had once deplored their windowless huts as symbolic of a determination to do evil), but because windows would weaken the mud walls and let in the cold. As for the fleas, I did not learn to love them but was willing to grant after a time that fleas, too, probably had their place in the divine plan. My vehement dislike for them began to seem like a wasted passion alongside the Indians' philosophical tolerance, for like hundreds of generations before them the Indians had cohabited with fleas and were not prepared to panic over them and spend hard-earned sucres on DDT just because the white man did.

I wished for every Indian a metal plow, a pair of good

oxen, better soil and pasture land, and for the Indians who were still held by white *patróns* as serfs, I wished freedom. Someday, I hoped, someone would come who could bring these things—someone trained in agriculture, husbandry, crop rotation, soil conservation. But these were not in my province and I had to accept things as they were. I hardly realized that this acceptance became less and less difficult for me.

My life went on alongside the life of the Quichuas. I do not say *with* theirs, for the two remained separate. All my efforts to make myself one with them ended at the brink of the great abyss—I was not an Indian. The topography of the land associated itself in my mind with this fact. The high sierras of Ecuador are cracked with huge abysses—*quebradas*, they are called, "broken places"—and no one can travel far in any direction without having to descend, bridge or skirt such ravines. My white blood could never become Indian blood, and therein lay the abyss which I could by no means descend, bridge or skirt.

For a time I adopted Indian dress. I bought from Pedro's wife Rosa two hand-woven woolen skirts and a shawl. In the town I found an embroidered blouse and a silver pin for my shawl. The shopkeeper supposed I was buying them for souvenirs—foreigners bought strange things as remembrances. But on the day that I first wore the clothes I met in the street the shopkeeper herself. At first she ignored me, thinking me an Indian, but then my height and gait told her that something was badly amiss. She shot me a look of horror which quickly changed to scorn.

It can't be helped, I said to myself; I didn't expect the whites to like the idea. One must choose the stratum of society with whom one will identify oneself, and run the risk of offending the others. (How had Jesus come to

[165]

choose the poor working class? I wondered. Might it not have been wiser to be middle class?) I had chosen the Indians and alienated the whites. The sooner I went on up the mountain where my friends were, the better.

The skirts felt very heavy and the blouse was uncomfortably baggy. The shawl scratched my arms. I could not get the pin to stay where I put it. Footwear presented the greatest problem. I had not been able to bring myself to go barefoot in such cold, and over such rough terrain. Impossible, I thought. But then the history of missions told of others who had become all things to all men, sometimes at great personal sacrifice. Hudson Taylor had grown a queue and worn a long Chinese gown. It never occurred to me that he might have minded doing this. When I had looked at the picture of my aunt in her sari I had thought it a very lovely and comfortable costume. But there were costumes which were not so comfortable or so becoming. This did not change the principle. Perhaps it was an unwillingness on my part, despite all I had proclaimed, to pay the price. What were cold feet—even bleeding feet—if they would make me a trifle less alien? But then I would not be able to walk so far, and perhaps even at all after a while. What could be gained? One must not go to extremes. I bought a pair of rope sandals, although women did not wear them. It seemed a sensible compromise. When I tried to walk in them, however, I was not convinced that they were an improvement over bare feet.

Rosa saw me coming and gazed in disbelief. I had told her when I bought the skirts that I was going to wear them, but the sight was a shock to her. A half smile played on her face—was this a kind of joke?

"*Buenos días*, Rosa," I said, but she was too absorbed to

[166]

reply. "I am a *runa* today." It was the name the Indians called themselves. It meant "person."

"You are wearing *runa* clothes for-no-particular-purpose?" She used the word *yanga*, a very useful word signifying the absence of a reason. It made a convenient reply to questions one did not wish to answer, and it was a way around explanations one did not wish to make. Rosa expected no better explanation than *yanga*.

"I wear them in order to be like you," I said.

"Like us?"

"Yes."

"You want to be like us?"

"Yes, Rosa. I want to be."

"And . . . your nice clothes? Did you throw them away?"

"No, I have them."

"What will you do with them?"

"Oh, I don't know. Sometimes, when I go to the city, I will wear them."

"Thinking to yourself, 'Today I am a white'?"

Yes. Rosa saw what it would be. A fake Indian one day, a white the next. There was hope notwithstanding that this measure might open some doors. But it did not prove to be so. Indians who did not know me met me with doubled suspicion. This foreign woman was clearly up to no good. Indians who knew me looked at me, I thought, with pity, as though commiserating with me over such a reversal of fortune.

"It's no good," said Pedro to me at last, when I had dressed like a Quichua for only a few days. "You are a señorita, but you look spoiled. You should dress like a señorita. It's no good for a señorita to become a *runa*."

Spoiled. It was the Indians I had thought of as the "unspoiled," but I saw now the unconscious irony of Pedro's words. He and the others of his tribe did not mean to refuse me admittance. They had accepted me from the beginning as a white woman. I must accept myself that way and not ask of them an impossible thing.

Nor should I, I reflected with some contrition, charge God with a botched job. If He had wanted the Quichuas won by a Quichua, He would not have sent them a white woman. It appeared that He *had* sent them a white woman. And God saw that it was good. Pedro's words helped me to see it, too.

"It's no good for a señorita to become a *runa*."

SUNDAY WAS visiting day among the Indians, and while some of them went faithfully to Mass in the church in town everyone spent the better part of the day going from house to house to talk and drink *chicha*, the sweet fermented drink made from corn or rice and occasionally rendered very festive by the addition of a pineapple bought in the market. There were always a few who succeeded in getting drunk and had to be pushed and hauled home, but *chicha* was not powerful enough to do much damage if drunk in ordinary quantities. Rosa made hers on Fridays and set it in clay pots by the door. She often gave me a glassful on Sundays when I would go to visit, and it became almost a habit for the children to beg me for a story as I sat on the little "porch" drinking my glass of *chicha* and listening to the other visitors talk. I had some Bible story books with large colored illustrations and I practiced my Quichua by explaining these pictures to the children and recounting the incidents that went with them. As soon as I arrived Jorge, instead of disappearing as he used to do, would inexplicably appear from nowhere.

"Señorita *shamun!*" he would whisper, "The señorita comes!" and any children present who did not know me

[169]

would dive for cover while Pava, Romero and Jorge, with any others who had satisfied themselves that I was harmless, crowded around.

"*Huillai, huillai*, señorita!" they begged, using the single Quichua word for "Tell us a story, tell us a story!"

"*Atiu!*" I would hear from the background—this was the expression of astonishment. "You mean she speaks our language?"

"She speaks it!" This was an overstatement, but children are easy to please, and I would begin, showing first a picture, then explaining it and asking questions to find out whether they understood. At times adult conversation ceased and I found everyone listening intently.

"Shut up! She's talking about God."

"About God?"

"Yes. That's the way she talks. Will it be for nothing, or will it be true? Who knows?"

Pava learned all the stories by heart and prompted me when I left out a detail. "No, señorita, not a goatskin—you said his mother put two kidskins on him to deceive his brother!" or, "You forgot to say that David cut off the giant's head—with the giant's own sword. Tell about that, señorita." And she would sit with her chin in her hand, her bright eyes darting from me to the other listeners to see if they were taking it in. Every now and then she would swat Jorge on the side of the head, whispering loudly, "What sort of a child are you, anyway? Shut up! Don't you hear the señorita talking?"

Romero would follow the movements of the story sometimes with pantomimes of his own—picking up five smooth stones and turning them over in his grubby brown hand, wondering, no doubt, if he could kill a man with those. When I tried to translate the Shepherd's Psalm for them, and described how the shepherd anointed the head with oil, I caught Romero rolling his eyes upward and shooting out his lower lip. Oil was a precious commodity, and involuntarily he tried to save it.

Pava persuaded her father several times to come and listen, although he probably felt that he had to listen enough on weekdays to my halting Quichua. Gradually, however, he took more interest in the stories.

"This is what your old fathers used to tell?" he asked.

"Well, yes, Pedro, my grandfather and my father told me these stories, but they learned them from a book, God's book. You know about that. Someday you and I are going to translate it into your language so your people will hear what God says."

"Is it for nothing that God speaks? Or is it true?"

"It is true, Pedro. It is not for nothing."

"It is a nice word. Your old fathers knew some good stories."

Rosa never actually came and sat down. When Pava asked her to listen she only fanned the fire more vigorously and said, "As if I have time to listen to stories!" When I asked her if she would like to hear, she gave me a faint smile and said, "I have to give my visitors *chicha.*" I suspected once in a while that she listened with one ear, forgetting herself when the story got absorbing and pausing in her work. She was busy at once when she found me looking.

Months passed, and I continued my weekday work and my Sunday visiting. I had told the story of Calvary several times, but there were some very important words missing—"to save" and "to forsake" were words I had not come across until one day when Rosa told me that while she was at the brook washing her clothes a friend's small child had fallen into the deepest place. By grabbing the child's foot Rosa had "saved" her. I had no sooner written it down than I heard Jorge crying outside and he burst into the house to tell his mother that Romero was going to take him to the lake to sail his reed boat. Between sobs he managed to say, "But Gustavo and Vicente came and Romero ran away with them and forsook me!" Rosa paid very little attention to the recital, and sent Jorge off to bring in some dried grass for the fire. I was overjoyed to learn the word, and the following Sunday I told again the story of the crucifixion of Jesus, quoting the mockers who said, "He saved others; Himself He cannot save," and trying to make clear to the Indians that the death of Jesus was that they might be saved. Pedro's cigarette grew a long ash as I told of Jesus' cry from the cross, "My God! My God! Why hast Thou forsaken me?" The ash fell on his poncho but still he did not move. I did not go on to the end of the story, and the Resurrection. I waited for Pedro to speak. Surely he had something to say this time, for his eyes did not leave my face.

"Señorita . . ."

"What is it, Pedro?"

"My brother is in jail. I was going to visit him today. Will you come with me?"

Pedro had mentioned his brother only once before, and I had not met him. Of course I would go.

The jail was on a tiny narrow street in Indi Urcu which had nothing to distinguish it from other side streets—there were doorways and a few windows on one side, a single double wooden gate set into high mud walls on the other. As we approached this gate a ragged little girl came slithering out from under it. An older girl was waiting nearby.

"Did you see her? What did she say about the money?" she asked the younger one. I could not hear the reply as the two went off down the street. There was a tiny square window in each half of the door, and a hand came through one of them.

"A little charity, señorita. Please, for the love of God a little charity."

Pedro banged on the gate and the face of a guard appeared at the other window.

"What is it?"

"I want to see Juan Chimbu."

"Who are you?"

"I am Pedro Chimbu, brother of Juan."

"Who is with you?"

"The señorita. The foreigner."

The gate opened and the owner of the hand, an old woman, pressed my arm, "A little charity, señorita," while the guard waved us inside. Several women hung around the gate, taking turns at the little window. They too were prisoners, Pedro told me, but they were allowed to beg and to see their children if the children were small enough to squeeze under the gate.

A game of volleyball was in progress in the open court-yard. The players seemed to be mostly of the *cholo* class. Three or four guards stood sleepily by. The one who had let us in led us through the yard into a passageway lined with cells, in each of which were two or three men or women. Most of them got up from their cots to watch us as we went down the passage. At the end of the first passage we came to a cement platform on which were some charred sticks and ashes.

"That is where the prisoners cook their food," Pedro said.

"They cook their own food?"

"If they have any to cook. When there is food, they cook it there."

"Does the prison not give them food?" I was incredulous.

"Sometimes they give them food. Sometimes the white prisoners get food. Juan doesn't get much. I brought him this." Pedro had a cloth bundle in his hand. The guard turned a corner and gestured toward a cell.

"There he is. What are you bringing him?"

"Some food, captain. Only a little food."

The guard took the bundle, opened it and dug into the cooked corn and beans with his hand, then handed it back to Pedro.

"Half an hour," he said, and left us.

Juan was sitting on a wooden bed with some sort of mattress on it, whittling on what looked like a flute. He looked up without speaking, and Pedro thrust the bundle through the bars.

"Good," said Juan. Pedro turned to me, feeling that something ought to be said, but all he could think of was "This is my brother, Juan." I greeted Juan and told him who I was, that I lived in the town, and I was a friend of Pedro and Rosa. He nodded and whittled. Another man sat behind him, on the other side of the bed, gluing together tiny pieces of wood to make a little toy dresser. He got up and brought one of the finished drawers over to the bars.

"Look, señorita. Would you like to buy this? I am making it to sell."

"He is here for debts," Juan volunteered, and Pedro joined in eagerly, as though he were the man's agent.

"Buy it, señorita Margarita! It is very nice."

The work was indeed skillful and my mind was again

filled with the old turmoils. The bleak prison, the dark cell, the hopelessness of getting out of debt, the numbers who were in similar straits, and here was this charming little piece of furniture, a bauble, a toy to cheer the heart—for a few moments—of some fortunate child. I said nothing. I had learned that an answer was not always required in this country and it spared me from having to think of a truthful and appropriate one. The three men glanced at each other. No one knew just how to pass the allotted half hour. Juan did not ask after Pedro's family or crops, and Pedro offered no information about Juan's. Finally Juan asked, "Have any of my children died?"

"No," said Pedro. "They live. Your wife lives."

Another silence. Then suddenly Pedro turned to me. "Tell a story, señorita." I was taken aback. Tell Juan a story?

"What story, Pedro?"

"The one you told at my house. About killing Jesus."

Juan whittled on his flute without speaking. The other man sat with the toy dresser on his knees, waiting to see what we would do. When I looked back later at that moment I wondered what made me hesitate. Had I failed utterly to grasp the implications of the opportunity? This was the very thing I had prayed and worked and schemed to achieve. But when the request came I saw it very simply —four people who were virtual strangers to one another (indeed, Pedro and Juan seemed hardly to be friends) who needed a way to pass the time. Quichuas loved stories— think of all the stories Pedro had told me. I obliged them by telling as much of the account of the crucifixion as I could with my limited vocabulary and time.

When I finished, Juan looked up from his whittling and said to Pedro, "Do you listen to that?"

[175]

"I listen to it," answered Pedro.

"She talks for nothing." Juan kicked away the shavings with his foot. "What is it worth, that talk?"

"Can it be for nothing? It is what God wrote, she says." Pedro spoke gently, not wishing to create an issue with his brother, nor to offend me. Juan's eyes narrowed and he ran the blade of his knife against the palm of his hand.

"That's what the priest says, too. He's always talking about that—about the Virgin and God and Jesus and Our Father and Christ and Our Lady and all those people. Who are they? Who knows them? Why talk so much about them?"

Juan's face was deeply lined, his hair matted, with a few strands of gray showing. He must be a good deal older than Pedro, I thought. I wonder why he is in jail? I had hesitated to ask Pedro, and he had given no hint as to the reason. His crime must be worse than the crimes of those who were playing volleyball in the courtyard.

The guard, a white man with a baggy khaki uniform and a gleaming badge on his cap, appeared and said, "Now." He gave Pedro a small shove and waved me toward the entrance. As we reached the courtyard a great cheer suddenly rose from the players—I thought it was the winning team congratulating themselves, but saw that the gate was opening and a man was leading two sheep into the prison. The game had stopped and the men looked hungrily at the animals. Today they would have meat. Would any of those in the cells share in it?

The guard looked us up and down before drawing back the bolt on the doors. He slammed them hard behind us and I heard the bolt grate in the slot. As we went silently down the sunny street together Juan's face stayed before me—much like Pedro's in its features, but older, more

[176]

suspicious, more willful and determined. Not that Pedro was anything but strong. He had a ruggedness about him that inspired my honest respect, but there was an openness that Juan did not seem to have, a tenderness with his children that I could not picture Juan displaying. But then, I told myself, I don't know Juan. Certainly I had seen precisely the same expression of suspicion and guardedness in Pedro's face on our first meetings in the market. He was not to be taken in any more than Juan. Perhaps Juan, too, would lay a hand softly on his little daughter's hair as I had seen Pedro do. Both men were members of a once proud race, a people of great intelligence and artistic sensibility. They had worshiped the sun, through which they had received warmth, abundance and life. They were defeated by a people who came to them in the name, they said, of the one true God—and in that name they plundered, betrayed and murdered. I thought of the prince, Atahualpa, shut up in a cell until his ransom—a roomful of gold—should be paid. And over the Andes came hundreds of llama-loads of precious ornaments and vessels of pure gold until the room was filled up to the mark on the wall. The Incas obeyed in good faith, confident that the price would release to them their leader. And then he was hanged, a kindness on the part of his captors, who had intended to burn him at the stake. With a Bible in one hand and a crucifix in the other, they had asked him if he would choose the true God, and he had consented and his punishment was mitigated.

There must be, of course, a just reason for Juan's being in prison. But if the white man had never come, what might he have been? I could not resist glancing sideways at Pedro, who walked a little behind me and to my right. What went on in his mind as he left his brother behind those walls?

[177]

What effect had Juan's attitude to my story had on him? Would he tell me what Juan had done against the law?

We did not go through the main plaza on our return. The less Pedro was seen in my company the easier it would be for him, I knew. There was a side street that would take me to my house and when we came to this I said goodbye unceremoniously so that Pedro could slip away without more ado. But it was then, for the first time since we left the jail, that he stopped in the street and spoke.

"Señorita Margarita," he said, "that word that you spoke —it is God's word, isn't it?"

"Yes, it is God's word."

"Juan doesn't believe that. But I, *I* believe it, señorita. It appears to me that the word is true. We ought to put it in my language."

"That is what I want to do, you know. That is why you have been helping me to learn your language."

"Good. I like that word. Juan, too, might like it if he saw it written on paper and knew that God said it."

He stood for a moment, pushing a stone with his toes, as though he had many things on his mind. Then he said, "Well, goodbye. You will be coming to my house soon?"

"Yes, on Tuesday, Pedro, as always. Goodbye."

As I turned up the street toward home I wondered if this was what it meant to be a believer. Pedro had said, "I believe it, señorita." If so, the angels in heaven must be singing. I should be singing, too, in the late Sunday quiet of the village street, but I did not want to make a spectacle of myself, even on the occasion of a soul's salvation, and I silently thanked God that He had not forgotten His promises.

16

NOT MANY weeks after our visit to the jail I was preparing to go to Pedro's house—this time not just for the usual language study, but to begin in earnest the translation of the Gospel of Mark. Long months of study lay behind me now, hundreds of pages of Quichua text had been analyzed, and the bits of Scripture which Pedro and I had translated had been read many times to the Indians. We needed more, a whole book, with its continuity and completeness, so I decided to begin with the shortest of the Gospels, that of Mark. I was just going out my gate in happy anticipation of the job when Mr. MacDonald's jeep came clattering up the road.

"I've brought a visitor to see you, Margaret," he said, climbing out. "This is Mr. Elmer Harvey of Millions Untold. He is making a mission survey in Latin America and wanted to see the work here in Indi Urcu." A beaming, heavy-set man in a raincoat bounded out of the jeep toward me.

"How do you do, Mr. Harvey." See the work, I repeated to myself. What work? Luckily, today there was something. "I was just going up the mountain to visit my informant. Do you think you'd like to come along?"

"Well, praise the Lord, Miss Sparhawk! Or can I call

you Margaret? No use being too formal. After all, we're all brothers and sisters in the Lord, isn't that right?" He laughed and shifted the camera straps a bit on his shoulder. "Your informant—sounds sort of sinister, doesn't it! You mean the one who helps you with language work?"

"Yes—I'm hoping to do a little translation work today."

"*Bible* translation?"

"Yes."

"Now isn't that wonderful! Guess the Lord brought us here on the right day, Brother MacDonald. Can't think of anything I'd rather do than go visiting with you, Margaret. Not sure I have just the right footgear"—he looked down at his shoes—"but it won't be too rough, will it?"

"It's dusty, and a bit steep," I said, "but I'm sure you can make it."

"Should have brought my old combat boots. They'd have been just the thing, but the airlines only allow you forty-four pounds. These new Florsheims weren't really made for rugged trekking. But then, nothing's too good for the Lord, eh, MacDonald? Ought to be glad to wear out a pair of shoes for Him!"

Mr. MacDonald gave him a thin smile.

"Could I give you a cup of tea before we leave?" I asked. Mr. MacDonald must be thirsty from the dusty drive up to Indi Urcu.

"Oh thank you, Margaret. If you have time, a cup of tea would be lovely," said Mr. MacDonald. This time his smile was warm.

Half an hour later we set out on foot for Pedro's house. The sun struck full on the eastern slope of Chimborazo, the great snowcap, setting it high and exalted above the whole earth, the joy of the valley beneath it. My heart lifted and cheered at the sight of that glory and seemed to run up the shining slopes.

"Cobblestones," said Mr. Harvey, picking his way carefully along the street in his polished shoes. "The genuine article. I suppose they've been here since the Year One."

"Maybe a hundred years," I ventured, not really having any idea how old they were.

We soon came to the end of the cobblestones and took the turn which led up the mountainside. Mr. Harvey, I noticed with some misgiving, was puffing already. The altitude might be too much for him.

"Turn around and look at the view from here, Mr. Harvey," I suggested, in order to give him a chance to rest. "Isn't the sun beautiful on the mountain?"

He paused, his shoulders heaving and making the two cameras rise and fall. He pushed his felt hat back a bit on his forehead, glanced at the mountain, and then looked down toward the village.

"Picturesque little place, isn't it? Wonder if I could get a picture."

Just then a small boy with two pigs came toward us on the road, one of the pigs grunting in time to his trotting, the other zigzagging back and forth across the road as the boy flourished a stick and yelled at him. Mr. Harvey looked apprehensively at the pig, which seemed bent on scurrying between his legs. The boy lunged at the pig, whacked it on the hind quarters, and sent it squealing past us.

"Say—there's a picture now. Could I get a picture of him?" He turned to me. I called to the boy and asked if the gringo might take his picture. The boy smiled shyly and nodded, but kept after his pigs.

"Do you think you could get him to stand over here on the sunny side, Margaret?"

"I'm afraid I can't get him to stand anywhere with those pigs. You'll just have to try to get them on the run."

[181]

Mr. Harvey was fussing with a light meter.

"Here. Over here I think the light will be perfect." He peered at the meter, then at the sky, then looked for the boy. He and his pigs were a block away.

"Oh say. That would have been a good one. Guess we'll have to let it go. Maybe I can get one of the town. Let's see. It is picturesque, isn't it, those mountains in the background and all. My. What a view." He looked through the range finder, turned the camera on end and back again, checked the setting, braced himself to snap the shutter, then turned abruptly.

"Oh—here. What's the matter with me? I want you people in this one. Would you mind standing over there by that palm tree—cactus, whatever it is? Both of you, if you don't mind. That's it. Little more to the left. That's good. I can see the whole town in back of you. That will be great." He snapped, grinned broadly. "Thanks a lot."

We walked up the road again. There was a slapping, beating sound, and we came upon a group of women in the meadow by the roadside, kneeling beside a narrow stream of water. Clothes lay all around them on the grass, stiff and humpy, drying in the sunshine. There were several flat rocks at the edge of the stream and over these the women bent, their *fachalinas*, the rectangular cloth worn around their shoulders, flung back, their breasts swinging in the loose blouses. Their hands were red when they lifted their arms out of the water, pounding the clothing into wads which streamed with water as they lifted them and slapped them down hard upon the stones. There was a rhythm in the bowing, slapping, lifting and bowing. It was broken for a moment as they paused to survey the foreigners with a direct, unabashed gaze. Mr. Harvey focused his camera and they bent to the task, their hair falling over their faces

[182]

again, the water shining and dripping from their arms. One woman was rubbing her hair with a handful of fibrous stuff which made it sudsy. She wore a dark blue cloth tied around under her arms in place of a blouse, and she dipped the glistening black mass of her hair into the icy water, where it waved and swirled in the current.

"How come they don't use any soap?" Mr. Harvey asked.

"It's too expensive for them, I suppose. And they pound the clothes so vigorously they must get most of the dirt out that way."

"How about giving them a tract?" said my visitor. "I have a bunch of Spanish tracts here." He dug into the pocket of his gabardine raincoat.

"I'm afraid they don't read. I doubt if they even *speak* Spanish," I told him.

"They don't read? Oh, I suppose not. But there'll be somebody at home who can read to them. Here, I'll just give them a few. They'll like it, and then it's seed sown. You never know what the results may be."

Seed sown. In Spanish. It would be like planting bananas in Alaska, I thought.

Mr. Harvey started to walk across the grass in the direction of the women. They looked at him apprehensively. All at once he drew up, lifting his feet one after the other and looking at his shoes. He had stepped into a bog, where the water from the stream had spread out into the thick grass. One of the women giggled, quickly covering her mouth with a wet hand. The others smiled furtively and went on washing.

"Guess it's no good going over there. They looked scared anyway, didn't they?" He tiptoed to firmer ground.

The road took us past cornfields and potato fields,

through pastures of grazing sheep and cattle, past a few huts which Mr. Harvey photographed. "Here. I'll have to get some of these thatched roofs. Really primitive, aren't they?" He snapped away, standing with feet apart and raincoat whipping in the wind, then winding his film with a tight-lipped smile of satisfaction. The smile faded as we walked and the powdery dust plastered his wet shoes. He stopped to scrape them on a tuft of grass, then took a clean handkerchief from his pocket and carefully wiped his forehead and the back of his neck. A glance at the color of the handkerchief afterward surprised him, and he quickly folded and stuffed it back into his pocket.

"Dust is terrific up here. How far is it to Pedro's?" he asked.

"Another half hour, perhaps," I told him. "We go by time rather than mileage up here."

"Pretty rugged climb. Do you do this often?"

"Two or three times a week."

"I guess we at home don't know much about what missionaries go through. And that's exactly why I came. I want to see what it's really like, so I can go back and challenge the rest of them." I could hear his breath coming in short gasps behind me for a moment. Then a wave of wind swept the sound away.

We reached Pedro's house and were greeted by the children, who had begun to look forward to my visits. Sometimes I brought them candy or small toys. Rosa was sitting on the porch weaving a *faja*, a narrow woolen belt. Mr. Harvey took a picture of her, after a futile attempt to get her to smile. She watched his movements in bewilderment, for although she knew what the camera was she did not know why he made faces at her. She went on with her weaving, telling us to sit down until Pedro came. He was

[184]

hoeing potatoes, but was expecting us and would soon be home.

We sat down, Mr. Harvey on a sack of corn, Mr. Mac-Donald and I on a bench that stood by the wall. A rooster raised a weak cry in the yard, and a couple of skinny hens scraped and picked about where he had been scratching. The valley lay in a veil of dust below us, but the mountain rose clear in the sun. I felt that we were set on a shelf midway between plain and peak. The breadth of this view never failed to gladden me, carrying my eye far down the slope up which we had come, across the wide plain, and up the smooth slopes to the east, beyond which lay the mystery of jungle and Amazon rain forest.

"Nice view up here too," said Mr. Harvey, tearing open a new roll of film. "Think I've about used up that roll, but I want to get Pablo when he comes—and you working with him, of course, Margaret."

Rosa got up from her weaving and went inside. Soon she appeared with bowls of soup for us.

"Do you think it's safe?" asked Mr. Harvey.

"Oh, I think so," said Mr. MacDonald. "I've eaten it many times, and never had any trouble."

"Well, I don't want to take any unnecessary risks. I've got a lot of trips lined up, and then I have to be back for deputation. They're just waiting for my report, you see. I'm not used to foreign foods. Of course, if I lived here like you do—" he broke off. Mr. MacDonald and I were drinking the soup, and Mr. Harvey took a tentative sip. Rosa was watching him closely. She had caught the tone of uncertainty in his voice when she offered it to him. He swallowed, looked at me, sniffed the soup and sipped again. He repressed the grimace he felt coming, and the soup was drunk without social disaster.

[185]

Finally Pedro came, his face and neck caked with dust, his clothes powdered to a uniform color. He picked up a rag from the floor near Rosa and wiped his forehead with hard, rough strokes as he greeted us. I knew that he had been working very hard, but he gave no indication that he was tired. He simply sat down on the doorsill, asked Rosa for a drink, and waited for me to start asking questions. I forgot for the moment what I was going to say. There was something in the frank, level gaze of his eyes—an almost innocent manliness—that made me feel a rush of pride and gratitude for him, and I wanted to say, "God bless you, Pedro." Instead, I said, "Today we are going to begin to translate God's word."

"It is so."

I had with me a copy of the New Testament in Spanish and English which I opened to the Gospel of Mark.

"The beginning of the Gospel of Jesus Christ, the Son of God." There was no noun for beginning. The infinitive could sometimes be used in this way, so I gave it a try. "Gospel" presented a problem. I found that it meant simply "good news" but Quichua had no word for news. How about "good word"? Pedro accepted that. There was no preposition "of." The idea had to be expressed as an adjective, as in, for example, "the tree foot" instead of "the foot of the tree," or as a possessive, "the tree's foot." So here it became "Jesus Christ, God's Son—about Him good word begins." Pedro said that was "hearable" all right, so I wrote it down.

"Could you just tilt your face a little bit toward the sun, Margaret?" said Mr. Harvey. "I can't quite get enough light on it. There. That's better. Now get Pablo to take his hand down so I can see the Bible. Oh, that's wonderful. I can even get a corner of the adobe wall and part of the

[186]

loom in." He clicked, wound, and clicked again. "Better take a couple, just in case."

We went through six verses of the first chapter of Mark in about two hours. There were no Quichua words for messenger, wilderness, baptize, forgiveness, confess, or camel. For each we had to employ a clumsy phrase, a Quichua approximation, or perhaps a Spanish loan word. The result of that first translation session left me feeling utterly deflated. How could I have thought I was prepared to undertake such a task? Two years was too short a time in which to know the Indian idiom sufficiently well to translate the Bible. I had read of missionaries doing it in less time than that—in fact, one missionary had learned a language and translated the whole book of Mark inside two years' time. How did they do it? I had seen pictures of them giving out copies of their translations to eager natives. Who taught the people to read? Were the translations really readable and meaningful? I looked over what I had just written and wondered if it would mean anything to an Ecuadorian Quichua.

"Well, Margaret, this has been a thrill for me!" exclaimed Mr. Harvey. "To think that God brought me here just on the very day you were to begin this great task. Now I can say I have actually seen and heard a missionary translating the Word of God. Wonderful, isn't it, MacDonald?"

The Scotsman did not quite manage to match Mr. Harvey's enthusiasm. He knew how far I was from success, though he did not belittle the attempt.

"It's a beginning, brother. It's a beginning." (And how many more beginnings will there have to be? I wondered gloomily. Surely this would all have to be done over, God knew how many times.) "She's got a long, hard job ahead of her, and of course there's no one, so far, who can teach the people to read Quichua. She'll have to do that, too, before the translation will be of any value."

"Yes." Mr. Harvey looked crestfallen. "I never thought of that. They don't read, do they? How about Pablo? Doesn't he read?"

"Pedro?" I said. "No, he doesn't read."

"Hardly anyone reads even Spanish. No one reads Quichua," said Mr. MacDonald.

"Is that right?" Mr. Harvey was amazed. "So you don't have a mission school here?"

"No. We had hoped to, but the couple who were assigned to establish it could not come."

"How about a church? You have a church here somewhere?"

"No, not yet."

"There must be one someplace among the mountain Quichuas—I mean, I'm sure I heard there was one someplace. Or was that in Peru?"

"There are one or two believers on stations north of here. You couldn't call them churches."

"What about medical work? Do you do any of that?" There was real anxiety in his tone now. Mr. MacDonald looked to me for the answer to this question. I explained as well as I could what I was doing, seeing the bewilderment grow in my visitor's eyes. Desperately he sought proofs, exhibits. What he had found was clearly not up to his expectations of the work of God.

"But in Guatemala we saw a tremendous work—why, there are so many believers among some of those tribes the witch doctors are going out of business! I saw a baptism of eighteen Indians—pure-blooded Indians—all on one Sunday, right there on the station. And schools, clinics, nice little

[188]

church buildings. But then you're just getting started, aren't you? Well, the Lord will work. Your labor is never in vain in the Lord, you've got to remember that."

The sun had passed its zenith and was sliding around to the west, throwing its rays now on the western slopes of Chimborazo. Pedro's children were peering out at us from the doors of the hut where they had been all during our visit.

"Don't these kids ever play?" asked Mr. Harvey.

"They seem to have little idea of playing as our children do. They work, and they can sit quietly much longer than American children can," Mr. MacDonald said. "I don't know why it is."

Mr. Harvey unsnapped his camera case again, but the children disappeared into the gloom.

"Shucks. Thought I could get a picture of them. They're so cute with their hats and ponchos and things. Won't they come out?"

I asked Pedro if they would mind.

"They are afraid," he said.

I suggested it was time to go, but Mr. Harvey was taking pictures again—of the pigs, the donkey, the view over the valley, Pedro with his rope sandals and dark poncho, the mud hut and the loom.

"I want to get all this stuff. I really want to be able to challenge the folks when I get back." He knelt on one knee to get a backlighted photo of Pedro against the sky, and the shoulder of the hill. I thought of possible captions Mr. Harvey might give it: "A typical Indian of the High Andes, one of millions still without Christ," or, if he chanced to catch Pedro smiling, "The light of the Gospel shines in the face of one of the descendants of the Inca sun worshipers." Challenge the folks back home. What did he mean? I had been "challenged" by men like him, had believed what they told me as though they had been oracles. Today I saw the makings of such a challenge—the swift, superficial glimpse; the intrusion it necessitated into two missionaries' time and an Indian's home; the frame of mind—Harvey had not come to learn but to document what he already assumed; his preconceptions governed his selection of picture subjects. Propaganda, I thought, demands simplification. Choose the pictures which show the poverty and primitiveness of the Indian, the successes of the missionary. Most disturbing of all to me was the realization that neither Mr. Harvey nor I was in a position to assess accurately either the Indians' need (who could say that they were worse off than New Yorkers, for example?) or my own success (who but God knew which were the victories, which the defeats?). For the visitor it was clearcut and simple: "Here is what God is doing." The picture of me with the open Bible and the earnest Indian, "Translating the Scriptures into the mountain Quichua dialect." It was fortunate, I thought with some irony, that Mr. Harvey had succeeded in finding one success of the kind he sought. What would he have done had I not been going to Pedro's that day? Lynn's formula came to my mind: Do the truth. How would Mr. Harvey have photographed that?

We said goodbye and I thanked Pedro and gave him his wages.

"Oh—you pay him for this?" Mr. Harvey was surprised.

"Why, yes."

"Wouldn't he do it without pay?"

"I don't know—but it's hard work for him. Harder than packing sacks of potatoes and firewood in the market."

"But isn't he a believer?"

"I think he is." The *non sequitur* puzzled me.

"A believer and he charges you for helping you translate the word of God?"

"Well—the laborer is worthy of his hire, isn't he? I wouldn't think of asking him to do it for nothing. He has his family to support. You see, Mr. Harvey, if he weren't working for me he would have to be working in the market, and I need him. He is unusually intelligent, I think, he speaks Spanish, and he was willing to do the work. All that means a great deal."

"Too bad, though, isn't it, that they won't do anything without pay. I suppose once you start paying them—well, it would be wonderful if they were willing just to serve the Lord." I thought of the meetings in which Mr. Harvey would show his pictures and of the offerings which would be collected for him just because he was serving the Lord.

We started down the mountainside, the wind flinging dust into our faces so that I could feel grit in my teeth. The cold penetrated our coats as the afternoon progressed. Some beautiful white birds sailed across the valley below us, brilliant against the somber color of the fields beyond them, and came to rest like neat, white boats on the lake.

"Do you see those lovely birds?" said Mr. MacDonald.

"Where?" asked Mr. Harvey.

"There. They've landed on the lake now, away down there."

"Oh. Yes. Pretty, aren't they? Wow, this wind is cold. Funny, you don't think of a country on the equator as being cold. Another one of the things folks back home just don't realize."

He would appear before his audiences as an authority. He had been there, he ought to know. And he could, in all honesty, present what seemed to him facts. Had he not incontestable evidence, there in his pictures, of the need of the Indian, and of the work of the missionary? Who would question the validity of the evidence? Who could gainsay him?

I watched the back of his thick neck, hunched into the raincoat, and heard his hard soles crunching on the stony earth. The cameras bobbed and swung at his side—packed with the evidence, I thought, for cameras "never lie"— material for a thousand illustrated "messages," thrill-packed missionary "challenges."

"Well, praise God!" said Mr. Harvey. *"Praise God!"*

CHAPTER

17

ONE DAY I took a new route home from Pedro's house,
going farther up the hill to the north, making a great circle,
through the fields, and coming down to the valley again to
the east. The sun shone brilliantly and the air was still and
warm, even on the highest fields. It was so unusual to
breathe dust-free air and to walk without being buffeted
by a cold wind that I went slowly, letting my eyes sweep
over the beautiful patchwork of the fields, reveling in the
world's loveliness as one does in the springtime after a long
bleak winter. High above the mountaintop nearest me I
saw a condor. I had never seen one before, but I knew him
from his likeness on the seal of Ecuador. His great wings
seemed to rest on the blueness and his head was bent over
the valley below him. A bird of incredible size, he wheeled
gently, tipping his wings almost imperceptibly, floating,
floating. I stood and watched him sail in the sky, the be-
reaved lover of the Quichua legend, but I thought of the
Spirit of God brooding over the face of the waters at
the creation of the world. And as He brooded above that
formless, empty darkness, He thought of light and He said,
"Let there be light."

Here it was. A glorious brilliance of light all about

me—on the snowcaps glistening in the distance, on the clouds that floated with the condor, on the white sheep that grazed a little way off.

God is light, and in Him is not any darkness at all. In the world He made, though, I thought as I walked along, there is plenty of it still—a great deal of darkness which does not seem to change very much. I had come here as a messenger of light, and for a long time had looked forward to the day when that light would begin to shine in Quichua souls. It occurred to me now that there was really nothing to mark the point at which I became an active missionary. Whatever transition there might have been between being helpless and helpful I had passed over without noticing. All that concern for preparation—what was it for? Perhaps there was, after all, no difference. If I had not noticed it, certainly the Indians hadn't. Had it made any difference to God?

The condor still floated in the sky. I could not see that he had changed his position at all.

I came presently to a hut where a girl was kneeling in the dooryard, grinding corn on a flat stone. Beside her on the ground stood a basket filled with ears of corn, and a great, flat clay plate with toasted kernels. She looked up at me, her black eyes wide with surprise at finding a white woman in her yard. She paused in her grinding, two small brown hands resting on the loaf-shaped grinding stone.

"*Buenos días,*" I said. "I am on my way home to the town."

"*Buenos días,*" she answered timidly. "To the town?"

"Yes. I live in Indi Urcu."

"You are the señorita that lives there."

"Yes. My name is Margarita."

"Mm."

"Your name? What is your name?"

"I am Manuela." The ease with which she told me, without giggling or hedging as so many of the women did, drew me to her. I wanted to talk some more.

"I come from Pedro Chimbu's house, where we have been translating God's word," I explained.

"God's word?"

"Yes. Did you know that God gave us a word?"

"No, señorita."

"Would you like to hear some of it, Manuela? I will read a little."

"Yes, señorita."

I sat down on the doorstep and she began again with her grinding. I read to her from the fifth chapter of Mark the story of the ruler of the synagogue, Jairus, whose little daughter was dying, and of how Jesus went to the house and found her dead and took her by the hand and said, "Little girl, I say to you, arise." And immediately the girl got up and walked.

"That child got up?" The stone came to an abrupt halt as the young woman asked the question.

"Yes."

"You said she was dead."

"Yes. She was dead. But Jesus, God's Son, came and caused her to get up."

"She got up alive?"

"Yes. Alive. Jesus can raise the dead, He can heal sick ones, He can do anything He wants."

"Where is He?"

"With His Father, God. He lives with God. But He wants to help us, too. He can help us if we trust Him."

"How can He help us? Where is He?"

This was more interest on the part of a woman than I

had met with for a long time, and we talked at some length about Jesus and what He wanted to do for any who would trust Him. I had a hard time explaining what trust meant, for the word I had to use was a Spanish corruption. Quichua had no such expression.

"You can trust Jesus. His word is a true word. You know that He will do what He says."

Manuela sat in silence, as though pondering whether there were such a person—one who would do what he says. I wondered if she understood the kind of faith I was talking about. She said she did. She began to wonder if Jesus could help her too. I did not jump at this as I once might have, aware now that her meaning could be any one of a thousand, and not necessarily indicative of the birth of saving faith. She went on grinding for a long time without speaking. Then she stopped pushing the stone and said, "My children are dead."

My heart sank. Did she want them back? I waited to hear.

"One child died when he was this size." She held her hand about three feet above the ground, fingers extended as though to shake hands, to show his size. "And the other miscarried. Now I am with child. Two months are yet lacking before he will see the light. Who will help me when he is born? He will perhaps die, too."

"I would be glad to come and help you if you wish."

"Can you make him live?"

"I don't know, but I will come and try."

"Can Jesus make him live?"

"Yes, Jesus can make him live if He wants to."

"Will He want to?"

"Perhaps He will want to. I will come if you call me, and

I will do whatever I can to help you. I will ask Jesus, too, to help you and to make your child live."

Leaning her weight on the grinding stone, Manuela searched my face. She had probably tried the witch doctor and the medicines. Whether she thought I could do no worse, or whether something gave her faith in me or even in God I could not tell, but she said, "I will call you, señorita."

Two months later I was awakened from sleep before dawn by a sharp rapping on my door. A child's voice called, "Señorita! Señorita *Gringa!*" I opened it, and found a boy of ten or twelve and a girl perhaps a year younger. "Manuela is giving birth," they announced. "She says come."

I asked them in, got dressed and collected what midwifery equipment I had and we started out.

The street was perfectly quiet at that hour, and the bare feet of the children padded softly on the cobblestones. The sharp night air cut into my lungs. A dog was barking far across the village, answered by others here and there.

As we climbed the hillside the great peaks of the Andes stood like black paper cutouts against the faintly paling sky. Two or three bright planets pierced the deep blue, and the moon, a half disk, floated above Chimborazo. Tufts of grass in the road crackled with frost as we walked.

We reached the hut to find Manuela on her knees facing the wall, her hands pulling on a rope which was strung from the rafters. Her husband, Victor, knelt behind her, lifting her under the arms as she rose and panted with pain. Several women stood about, and her mother, a toothless old Indian with a blue cloth on her head, squatted on the floor beside Victor, instructing him in an urgent whisper to keep lifting, keep lifting. Then she turned to Manuela and said, "Hard now. As hard as you can. Do not stop. *Hard*." The old woman moved over and tightened the woven belt around the girl's waist. This, I learned later, was to keep the child from coming out the mother's mouth.

I asked if everything was all right. Yes, they said, but— someone thought to add, quite casually—perhaps the baby would come feet first. One of the women then insisted that she was sure it would, for Manuela had sheared a ewe that had died during the new moon, and this, all women knew, was taboo during pregnancy.

"I tried to get her to light a candle for our saint, but she would not hear," said the old mother. "Now the child will be born head up and will die."

I went over in my mind all that Lynn had taught me about the procedure for delivering a breech. Only the simplest measures would be possible under these circum- stances, but they might be life-saving. I asked that some water be heated and cloths collected. The Indians listened solemnly to my requests but no one hastened to carry them out. They argued among themselves as to who should do it and whether it was worth the trouble.

"What will she do?" they asked one another. "She will not make it live, will she? How can she make it live?"

I found a place on a pile of sheepskins and sat down to wait, since neither Victor nor his mother-in-law seemed willing to relinquish his place to me. Lynn had told me it was useless to insist that a woman in labor lie down unless there was an emergency, since the Indians believed that birth took place by sheer gravity, with a good deal of squeezing and shaking by the husband when the mother's strength ebbed.

It was a long day. I sat through the rest of the morning,

as the sun climbed above the valley and threw its rays into the courtyard between the mud walls, and then as it passed, in the afternoon, toward the Pacific and left the little house in darkness once more. At intervals Victor gave up his task of jerking and jiggling and sat down on another pile of skins to drink his corn soup or chew a mouthful of *máchica*. No one thought of offering Manuela any sustenance until I asked Victor if she might not have some *máchica*, too. He went over and pushed a spoonful of the dry, toasted barley flour under her tongue.

The women sat gossiping, recalling other births they had witnessed wherein mother and baby lived, or the mother died, or the baby died, and they told the details of birth and death with equal relish, while Manuela knelt and sweated by the wall, rising and sinking, crying out in a small voice once or twice, silent the rest of the time. I sat and prayed, listened to the women, tried to talk to Manuela to encourage her, played a little with the two children who had fetched me, and prayed again.

"God save Manuela. O Lord, help her, let her live." But she'll live, I told myself. Nothing wrong, probably. Birth is a normal process.

I looked at Victor, gulping his soup in the corner. He was obviously not worried. Even the old mother, though she urged Manuela intermittently to keep working, was placid enough about it. I had learned a lot from the Indians about accepting life calmly, and the lesson had given me a cooler view of my own hardships and even of my own importance. If my alarm at what had originally seemed the deplorable condition of the Indian had diminished, my sense of being needed by them had diminished correspondingly. Manuela will be all right. No need for any desperate praying yet.

[199]

But, Lord, You must have brought me here for some reason. Show me what it is. Show me that I am needed for *something*.

Manuela let go the rope and sank back on her heels, letting her head drop into her hands. "*Aylla*," she said in a whisper, a Quichua expression of woe.

"What's the matter with you?" her mother asked sharply. "Get up there. It's no good sitting down. Get up."

Manuela wiped the sweat from her forehead with a corner of her shawl, rose to her knees again and pulled on the rope. I could not imagine how she had an ounce of strength left. The lack of concern on the part of all present disturbed me. It was all very well to accept life and its conditions without complaining—I had been pleased to find that the crises need not be turned over to the professionals as I had been taught to think. Birth, marriage, accidents, old age, death—all these things were dealt with by the people themselves, in the sanctuary of home as a part of the course of life, not to be interfered with by outsiders, and whatever might be said for the other side, the Indian way seemed laudably humane and in harmony with nature.

But as soon as I heard another cry from Manuela, my philosophizing stopped and I began to think that something must surely be amiss or the baby would have been born by now. Perhaps the women were right—the baby was right side up, and Manuela was in trouble. Something ought to be done. Someone at the very least should be concerned about her.

Lord, give me wisdom. If something ought to be done, show me what it is. Should I do it now? Suppose I delay too long? On the other hand, the Indians are all calm enough. I must not make a fool of myself by declaring an emergency where none exists—I could alienate them.

Manuela sat back once more. "Not yet," she said.

"Not yet?" said the old woman.

"Not yet."

I felt as though everyone drew a slight breath of relief. Perhaps it was only I. How foolish of me to become so agitated by physical suffering when it was the spiritual needs I should have been most deeply concerned about. Had my sense of the Indians' spiritual plight been dulled by familiarity? Probably it had. But whose fault was that? How can the human spirit be held taut for years? Are we not created with resiliency so that we can support the tensions of life? God had given me a task to do in the translation work at least, if not in the area of evangelism. As for the latter, perhaps I had not appropriated the power of God as I ought to have, or perhaps I was never intended for that job, and the sooner my definition of my task was pared down to the size God meant it to be, the better. I hoped with all my soul that I was not to blame, but admitted the possibility that I was, and the burden of guilt became intolerable when I thought that not only was I to be cast aside as unusable, but the millions of Quichuas whom I had taken upon my heart were now without an intercessor. God could do nothing with *me*, and there was no other.

I was not allowed to resolve the hopeless tangle of reasonings. Victor had left the house to get water from the aqueduct half a mile away when Manuela suddenly said, "*Shamun!*" "It is coming!" and reached for the rope.

Things worked better than my highest hopes. The baby was indeed head up as the women had predicted, but I prayed, "Lord help me *now*—let me do this much for them," and then I did what Lynn had taught me, the baby's life was saved, Manuela lay back exhausted and grateful, the women looked at me in wonder. Breech babies never, they said, survived. The pulling and hauling they did would have killed the child, I supposed, if the delay had not first suffocated it, so this to them was a miracle.

Nothing had been prepared for the child, for even if everything had gone smoothly the chances for survival were about equal with the chances of death, so the Indians had hardly thought it worthwhile to take any trouble beforehand. Better to wait and see what the results were. So now they had to rummage through the piles of rags, blankets, and skins to find something to wrap the baby in. Some cloths were finally found, the child was wrapped and then bound round and round with *faja* belting, its little arms pinned firmly to its sides, its legs straightened and pressed together. Then it was laid on the sheepskins like a tiny mummy next to its mother.

CHAPTER

18

⌇

I HAD been up this mountain many times during the day, but never during a night of pouring rain and roaring wind. By this time the rain was seeping through the coat that was supposed to have been waterproof, and water ran down my neck. "Are they servants of Christ? I am a better one—I am talking like a madman—with far greater labors. . . . Three times I have been beaten with rods; once I was stoned . . . adrift at sea; on frequent journeys, in danger from rivers . . . through many a sleepless night . . . in cold and exposure." The Apostle Paul had listed his hardships, not pretending that he had never made a sacrifice. I might list one or two of my own. I felt exhilarated by the wildness of the night, the streaming, slashing rain, the screaming, lashing wind. But why hadn't the man at least brought a light? My flashlight was feeble, and since I had given it to him to carry I walked mostly in darkness.

The man had come to my house late that night to say that his little daughter was desperately ill with what seemed to be poisoning. Word had run from hut to hut over the mountainside that Manuela had given birth to a feet-first baby, and that the white señorita had made it live, and since that time increasing numbers of Indians found their way to my door in Indi Urcu. Sometimes they came under a pretext of selling me something but often it was with the frank request for medical treatment of one kind or another, or with a plea that I come to visit a sick relative.

Here was another one. The idea of treating such an emergency frightened me—my reputation as a miracle-working midwife did not qualify me for this job, but I did not see how I could refuse at least to attempt assistance. I found an emetic, which I put in the bag with the other standard remedies, and we started off as fast as we could up the mountainside.

The night was perfectly black and the trail soon became a rushing river of water. I could feel the water squelching in my shoes, and apart from the knowledge that they would be ruined I rather enjoyed the memory of childhood puddle splashing that the cool wetness evoked. The trail, however, became more and more slippery as we ascended and I could not see whether I was putting my foot down on a rock or on greasy clay. The effort of trying to keep up with my guide, who was understandably in a hurry, and seeking a foothold at the same time tired me quickly. How far would it be? I knew it was useless to ask—time and again the Indian estimate ("Just over that hill" or "Now we are in my dooryard") had been wide of the mark. I hunched my shoulders up higher to keep the rain from trickling down my neck and hoped most earnestly that this journey would not be in vain.

There was a time when "in vain" to me had meant that there was no visible spiritual result. A study of the public life of Jesus convinced me that he regarded things differently, since comparatively few of his encounters with individuals or groups resulted in manifestations of true faith. I still wanted proof of my effectiveness in some area, and the success with Manuela had been gratifying. Perhaps God had not intended to draw her or her immediate family to Christ through that cure, but at least He had given the physical evidence of His power, and there was reason to hope that spiritual results might ultimately follow. All my life I had been conditioned to regard every chance conversation, every accident by which my path crossed that of another human being (especially if that human being was a stranger—people I knew somehow fell into a different category) as God's way of thrusting in some truth. During the past two years this dream had suffered some revision which, as I hurried along in the dancing fragments of light thrown by my guide's flashlight, I tried to define. What had taken place? Originally I was a missionary with the broad scope of service that the name implied in my thinking: to win souls, to translate the Scriptures, to use medicine and education for the sake of the Kingdom. Then I accepted the role of mere translator—I was prepared for that, I seemed to do better at it than at evangelism, and the task was so demonstrably the work of God. In recent months, however, I had been reluctantly a doctor. The Indians had finally discovered a use they could make of me, and although I dreaded the thought of becoming a quack and studiously avoided advertising my medical skills, there was no escape from duty which presented itself at my door.

We were skirting the edge of a *quebrada*. The wind scooped down into the ravine and rushed upward into our faces, slapping sheets of water against us and tearing at our soaked clothes. It was such a journey as I had never made before, and I thought it would have fit quite nicely into St. Paul's catalogue. His sufferings resulted in triumph. Lord, let this trip, too, at least be worthwhile. I don't mind losing sleep and a pair of shoes if I don't lose the patient or the opportunity to speak of Christ. If Jesus did not always gain a disciple, at least He healed the sufferer who came to Him. Which would it be tonight?

The roar of wind and water made talk impossible, but at last the Indian turned and shouted, "There is my house over there—do you see the light?" I could not see any light, but I thought I could hear another sound above the swish of the wind. The Indian heard it too, for he stopped short, leaning into the wind, and then, the flashlight making a swift arc in the fog, he threw his hands to his head. "Already dead."

It was the death wail that we heard, a wild, hopeless song lament reaching us in waves through the rain.

He resumed his steps, more slowly, and we reached the house to find the mother rocking the child, limp and still in her arms, and a crowd of people shrieking and keening in despair. They stopped long enough to recount the last moments, and I stayed to try to comfort them with the words of Him who said, "I am the Life." But they were in no mood to listen to talk of any kind. It was not talk they wanted. The child was dead; the white woman had not come in time; it was all over. I might have spoken to them, have pronounced a verbal prescription for their need, but I saw that I had no right to presume on their plea for help. They had wanted me to save a life. I had failed to do that; I could go now. No matter what I had to say, what other offers I might make, it was over. The one thing they had wanted from me they had not gotten.

One of the children was sent to guide me home again, and as I walked, still in lashing rain and wind, still in darkness, I told myself that I was not to blame. Clearly I had done what I could. The child could not in all probability have been saved if I had arrived in time—even a doctor loses patients and this child had not been my patient. God knew I had had nothing to do with her death. But if He knew that, He knew ahead of time that she would die. Why this useless frantic race up the mountain in the mud and rain, in the middle of the night?

For nothing. For nothing. For nothing. The rain came in increased force, sending stinging scourges against me. If only this *rain* would stop—now that the job was over, the trip seen to have been fruitless, what was the point in having to keep up the struggle just to get home? I slowed down a little, for there was no reason for urgency now. Still the rain beat down.

A few days after Manuela's delivery I had written a circular letter, asking my friends to pray for her spiritual enlightenment. It was satisfying to be able to recount the medical success, and to tell them of the completion of the translation of the Gospel of Mark—Pedro and I were now working on Genesis, and he had shown real interest in the Scriptures and understanding of the task we were jointly engaged in.

If I were to write of tonight's incident, what would I say? The rain swiped at me, as though a troublesome Providence nagged for my attention when I wanted to focus it even for a moment on my own anxieties. Thoroughly drenched anyway, I resolved to ignore the storm and pursue my thoughts.

Medicine, I had understood, was to be used as the servant of missions, a means for bringing the masses under the "sound of the Gospel." Why didn't it work for me here? Lynn's clinic, the vaccination of the school children, my countless visits, the giving away of hundreds of sucres' worth of drugs, even the resounding success of Manuela's childbirth had produced hardly a single exhibit to prove that medicine was a means to the great missionary end. And if it is an end in itself, I thought wryly, what business have I to be involved in it without proper training? Lynn was legitimately involved—she was a doctor.

But then, of course, if I were to write in my next circular about tonight's journey, I couldn't put it in either category. It was nothing, really, except an adventure—it would seem an adventure to my friends at home, though right now it was sheer misery.

"Are you coming, señorita?" The child was far ahead, and had stopped to call back. I tried to quicken my pace a little but the effort was too great.

"I'm coming," I said.

Why this need to find meaning at every turn? Why do I struggle to sort out the material and the spiritual, to separate the failures from the successes? Well, if you're going to write honest prayer letters . . . That was what tormented me.

I thought of that sunny afternoon when I had traveled down this path with Mr. MacDonald and Mr. Harvey, appalled at the ease with which Mr. Harvey assessed the work of the Lord—these are the victories, these are the defeats. Who was I to label things?

The rain had subsided to a gentle whisper, and I could hear the quick little splashes of the child's feet in the water which still flowed in the trail. By the time we reached my gateway the sky over the eastern cordillera had grayed. The night was past.

"Will you come in and have a cup of coffee?" I asked my little guide.

"*Bueno*, señorita." She followed me inside and I set

about finding something to eat with the coffee. I was suddenly aware of a ravenous hunger.

"Whether therefore ye eat, or drink . . . do all to the glory of God." St. Paul had recognized even the common things. Of course I knew that; I had heard sermons on it. But I saw now that if my task was far smaller in terms of the effect it was to produce, it was far larger in terms of my own life involvement. If there were times when I must be willing to pay any price for what was called the "advancement of the Kingdom" there were also times when I must be willing to let such a price—climbing a mountain, for example, in rain and mud and darkness—be paid in vain. This, too, was a place to glorify God. This must have been what Lynn meant, I thought as I set the table. "Jesus told us to do what is true."

THERE WAS no reason to forge ahead with translation of the Bible, I realized, unless there were readers. And there would be no readers unless I myself taught them. Willy-nilly, I found myself involved in education as well as in medicine and translation. As Pedro and I would sit translating, Jorge and Romero would often hang over my shoulder. In the story of Jacob and Esau I needed a word for "game." I explained to Pedro that it meant meat gotten in the field or forest, not guinea pig or sheep as they were used to. Pedro scratched his head and finally decided that there was no other word for meat. Meat was meat. *Aicha.* I wrote it down, and Jorge said, "She writes *aicha.*"

"Where?" said Romero.

"Where, señorita, where is *aicha?* There?" said Jorge.

"Yes," I said. "This part says *ai,* this part says *cha. Aicha.*" Quichua is a simple language, well-adapted to teaching reading by syllables, and it was not long before the two boys had mastered the three vowels and most of the consonants and could put the syllables together.

My work with Pedro, along with the new reading lessons and my continued medical visits to many homes made it necessary for me to spend a great deal of time walking back and forth from the town. That endless trudge in the rain convinced me that I ought to move closer to the Indians. It would be hard to give up my little house, but how could I stop at the price if such a move would mean closer contact with the Indians? Not that I believed, at this point, that I would ever succeed in identifying myself with them. Nor did I any longer see this as of any great importance. The Indians had become people to me—they were no longer my "field." While I had once declared them to be my equals, I now regarded myself as theirs. Instead of saying, "Oh, you are as good as I—let me help you," I now said, "I am as poor as you. God help us all."

During the first year in Indi Urcu I had coveted the privilege of making noticeable sacrifices—the comfortable village house was one I hoped to make. It was too nice, really, for a pioneer missionary. But at the time there was no way of doing it. Ironically, now that I had learned to be content with lesser self-denials, I saw the opportunity of giving up the house. Pedro told me of an empty house not far from his which could be cleaned up and used if I wanted to put a little money into new tiles for the roof and a new door frame. A young Indian had contracted tuberculosis and been sent to the government hospital, leaving his wife and two small children to run the farm. They had struggled with it but finally given up and gone home to her parents, leaving the house empty and the fields untilled. If I would live in the house Pedro said he would arrange for an Indian to take care of the potato crop. The small rent for the house would cover his wages and the owner would not lose his land. It took some time before the arrangements could be worked out. I looked forward to the move, for funds had been dropping off somewhat of late, and it was expedient for me to look for cheaper quarters. None of my

[211]

supporters had written directly to explain the decrease in gifts, but one or two had expressed, if not distress, surprise at my sympathy for the Indian outlook. I inferred that they took this as a questioning of the traditional missionary outlook. I searched my form letters for hints that the mission's program was anything but unimpeachable, and found nothing.

Romero, Jorge and Pava had made great strides in reading Quichua. The language had only three vowels, and teaching by syllables was comparatively simple. It was quite another thing to teach them to read with any indication of the sense of the words. The mere idea that the words were supposed to *mean* something was new to them, but Romero finally understood and one day I asked him to read aloud from our translation of Mark so that his mother could hear. Up until this time she had paid little attention to the reading lessons, willing enough to let the children learn whatever it was I wanted to teach them—perhaps because it pacified me as well as them—but ignorant of the purpose. Today I announced to her that the children would read from God's word and she must listen. Obligingly she stopped her work. Romero began to read.

"And they brought him to the place called Golgotha (which means the place of a skull). And they offered him wine mingled with myrrh; but he did not take it." Romero had trouble pronouncing the Spanish words we had introduced for the name of the hill and the myrrh. Here Rosa interrupted.

"This is God's word?"

"Yes," I said, pleased that she had remembered that.

"God speaks Quichua?"

"Yes," I said, "He speaks your language. Men wrote His book in another language and we translate it" (the

[212]

Quichua word meant "to take across") "into your language. Pedro and I have been translating it, and now your son can read it."

The boy went on. "And they crucified Him, and divided His garments among them, casting lots for them, to decide what each should take." Again Rosa stopped him.

"Is he reading? Is he reading the paper?"

"Yes," I replied, even more pleased that she had recognized the skill. "Romero is reading the paper. This is what I have been teaching your children all these weeks. It is not easy to read, but Romero has learned, and now he reads God's word for you."

"He is reading Quichua!"

I was delighted. "Yes!" I said. "Quichua."

Rosa's face grew dark and suspicious. "But he *knows* Quichua. Why did you teach him to read Quichua?"

Her anger stunned me. Was she not pleased with Romero's new ability?

"But, Rosa—" I began.

"Why did you not teach him to read Spanish? When people read, they read Spanish. What good is it to read Quichua? Quichua! We are Quichuas! As if he did not know Quichua!" She tore the paper from his hand and flung it toward the fire. Pava snatched it up and clutched it to herself defensively, her eyes snapping like her mother's. "I want my children to *learn*," Rosa went on. "I want them to learn like the white man, to know what the white man knows. Why would I want them to learn Quichua?" She got up from the floor and began violently throwing corn cobs into a basket. Pedro picked at the frayed rope of his sandal. I waited for him to speak, but he said nothing.

"Do *you* understand, Pedro?" I asked.

"Yes, I understand."

[213]

"Why did we translate God's word?"

"To take it across from Spanish."

"And why did we take it across from Spanish?" Oh Pedro—if you don't know the answer to this one, after all this time . . .

"To put it into our own language, so that we Quichuas could hear it."

"And you see why I taught your children to read in Quichua, and why I want you to learn?"

"So that we could read what God says, señorita."

"So that you could read what God says. He wants to speak to you."

Pedro picked at his sandal for a while. He pulled out a fiber and began to run it through his teeth. Then he looked at me and said, "Has God not spoken in Spanish?"

"Well, Pedro—you know He has. You know we use the Spanish God's Word—what do you mean?"

"If He has spoken in Spanish, we will hear Him in Spanish. It is enough."

"But, Pedro, we have talked many times of how each man needs to hear it in his mother's tongue."

He considered this for a moment, pensively running the thread through his teeth. Then he spat in the fire and said, "No. It is enough, señorita. The white man hears it in Spanish. We, like the white man, will also hear it in Spanish."

"WHO KNOWS where he will be?" Rosa picked up a huge, flat plate made of clay and set it evenly on the three hearthstones. "Will you wait for him?"

"Yes," I said, disappointed at not finding Pedro at home this afternoon, but unwilling to put off any longer the matter about which I had come to speak.

"Sit down, señorita. Coming he will come. Probably very soon." She began rubbing fat kernels of dried corn off the cobs into the plate. "Pava! The spoon."

The girl climbed onto some sheepskins and pulled a long wooden spoon from the thatch roof. *"Hün."* With the nasal grunt which means "Here!" she extended the spoon toward her mother over the plate. Rosa took the spoon and began pushing the corn around and across the plate, turning it over slowly, scraping the clay dish with a soft woody rhythm. A solemn boy of about three—the child who had been on her back when I first met Rosa—sat near her on the mud floor, tapping a corn cob on a piece of broken pottery.

"To translate God's word you come?" Rosa looked at me through the smoke, brushing back a lock of dusty hair with her left hand, never pausing with the stirring.

"No, Rosa, not today. I came today to talk to Pedro."

"*Yanga?* Did you come to talk *yanga?*" She used again the word which means for-no-particular-purpose. It used to infuriate me, and I had at first refused to use it myself. It seemed evasive, senseless, and, for me, a lie. I did not do things *yanga*. God willing, the Indians, too, were going to learn to have some purpose in life. Today, however, I was tempted to agree that I had come for nothing. It no longer seemed like a lie to me, for it was the Indian way of saying all that needed to be said. The Western compulsion to account for everything struck me now as pompous and at times defensive. On the other hand, I may as well tell her my reason for coming, I thought. Not that she will be of any help, but it will make conversation, and this is difficult enough with Rosa.

"I came to talk about the house."

"Oh. The house you want to live in?"

"Yes."

She snatched a kernel of corn from the hot plate and tossed it quickly in her hand, patting it against her mouth for a second, then dropped it back into the plate.

"Your house in the town is no good? You don't like to live there?"

We had been over all this, and I did not know how to make Rosa understand any more than I had already told her.

"It is far away. I have a long way to walk to get to the *runa* houses, and I would like to live near you."

"Oh." She put a corncob between the stones and blew on the fire with a hollow straw. Taking the spoon again, she went on stirring. "You want to live near us, señorita."

"Yes."

"Are you ever going back to your own land?"

[216]

"I don't know. I suppose I will, someday, to visit."

"Your mother lives?"

"Yes. And my father."

"And do they not say come?"

"Oh yes, they want me to come home to visit."

"Not to stay?"

"No. My parents want me to do what God wants, and I think God says I should live here."

"Are you going to get married?" She picked up another kernel and tested it as she had before, then crunched it between her yellowed worn teeth, watching me through the smoke.

I laughed. "Oh Rosa, how many times have you asked me that? I don't know, I told you. I don't know if I will ever get married."

"Don't they ask for you? Don't your kind of men ask?"

"No, Rosa. They don't ask."

She scraped some toasted corn from the plate into a basket and rubbed off more kernels to toast. "Pava. Give some *tostados* to the señorita."

Pava came and picked up the basket, brought it over to where I sat. "Do you like these?" she asked timidly.

"Yes. Oh, I think they're very good. We didn't have this kind of corn in my country."

"Is that true?" Rosa looked up in surprise. "What kind of corn did you have?"

I knew very little even in English about varieties of corn and tried to think of a way to describe them in Quichua. When would Pedro come home? Waiting. Always waiting, marking time, wondering when things were going to start.

"Oh, it was a smaller kind than this. We did not have big—" I could not think of the word for kernel—"the big kind that you toast." Would Pedro have been able to get

[217]

me the house by this time? Why didn't he come? He was usually home by this hour.

"What kind do you toast in your country?"

Oh dear. What kind did we toast? Rosa, how am I to explain to you. Why doesn't Pedro come?

"We don't toast corn in my country."

There was a stirring and snuffling in the corner that did not come from the guinea pigs.

"Pava. Bring the baby." Pava rose, went over to the corner where a white cloth was slung between the walls, and stood on tiptoe, her delicate little ankles exposed beneath the cherry-colored wool skirt, the soles of her bare feet showing gray in the smoky light. With some wrestling she extracted the baby from the hammock, draped him over her shoulder, and handed him to his mother.

"You don't toast corn in your country." Rosa sat back with one heel curled under her, one neat small foot stretched out beside the fire, and laid the baby across her lap. He burrowed furiously under her blouse, found what he wanted, and let his feet flop in contentment. His small snortings and smackings mingled with the scraping of the spoon and the rattle of the corn. Firelight, shelter, food to eat, love. You don't know what you've got, Rosa.

"What do you have?" Rosa asked.

I was about to say "Nothing," when I realized that Rosa's question bore no reference to what I was thinking just then. What was it? Corn. We had been talking about not having corn in my country.

"Oh, we have other things. Lots of other kinds of food."

"And if you live near us, you will eat *runa* food?"

"Of course, Rosa! I like *runa* food."

Rosa lifted the plate off the fire and dumped the batch of

[218]

tostados into the basket. "You will like it, perhaps. You will not like it, perhaps."

"But I do like it, Rosa. I have eaten all kinds of *runa* food."

"Food! I am talking about the house. Who knows if you will like the house? Who knows if Pedro will get it for you?"

Was there some reason for putting me off from week to week? Each time I had asked him, Pedro had had some reason for not being able to get the house for me. I had offered an increase in the rent I originally proposed and still he put me off. Was it that they did not want me to live near them? I did not really expect them to urge me to come. My presence could hardly have so much importance to them.

There seemed to be nothing to say, and I sat watching the guinea pigs scuffling around the floor. Pava tore bits of leaves from a basket by her side and fed them, careful to give them equal portions. The three-year-old made passes at them with a corncob to hear them squeal.

"Wait for the Lord; be strong, and let your heart take courage; yea, wait for the Lord!" I've been waiting, Lord. Waiting and waiting. Not just for Pedro this afternoon. You know I waited a long time to be a missionary to mountain Indians. Then I waited for the Gardners. They didn't come. Then I waited to see what I was to do next, and You seemed to say translation and medical work. So you gave me Pedro—I don't discount that answer to prayer, Lord, or Manuela's baby. I don't want to belittle Your faithfulness to me. Just being here today, I know, is an answer to prayer. Think what it took. Kindness of friends, help from home, encouragement of people like the

[219]

MacDonalds, support that is still coming in (it's probably good for me not to have so much—keeps me looking to You. If I skimp—if I can just get that Indian house—I will be able to live much more simply), prayers of many friends—all these things, good and perfect gifts, coming down from the Father of Lights. I don't complain against You now, Lord—just show me the way. Nothing very startling has happened—maybe it's not supposed to. Let me be content with whatever You want. Just bring Pedro back now, please, for one thing. It gets pretty boring sitting here. Smoke gets in my eyes. My back is tired. There's no school yet, either, Lord. What am I to make of the Indians' attitude toward the translation and learning to read Quichua? There's no visible change *anywhere*. Pedro? What about Pedro? Oh yes, perhaps he is a Christian. I certainly hope so; I trust so. But then, Lord, he is in my pay. No souls to claim, really. No stars in my crown, no figs on the tree.

"Father is coming." Pava jumped up and went to the door. "The señorita is here," she called. "Come quickly. *Atsai!* Mama . . . what is the matter with father?"

"What is it?" said Rosa, looking up sharply.

"Why does he walk that way?"

Rosa lifted the baby in her arms and rose from the floor, peering out into the blinding sunlight of the fields.

"Jesús Santa María, his leg is bad again. It is for that he did not come quickly. *What is the matter with you?*" She shouted at him, not calling his name. I had never heard her address him by name. I got up too, and saw Pedro stumbling across the potato fields toward the gate in the mud wall, his trouser leg rolled up, his hand clutching a rag with which he stooped once to wipe his leg.

"What happened to him, Rosa?" I asked.

[220]

"He gets that way *yanga. Yanga* his leg becomes worse."

Pedro came into the house, limping to the bed in the corner.

"*Buenas tardes*, señorita."

"*Buenas tardes*, Pedro."

"Did you bring your needle, señorita?"

I had been earlier that day to visit a child with an infected hand and had with me my penicillin and syringe.

"Yes, I brought it."

"Stick me, please, señorita. It hurts badly."

"What is it, Pedro? What did you do to your leg?"

"It's just that way. It gets well, and it gets bad again. Pus comes out, it hurts badly, I can't walk. Today I was working in my cornfield and it hurt more and more and I worked more and more and then I felt my trousers sticking to my leg when I bent over like this, and I looked at my leg and it had pus coming out, pus running down my leg, and my leg is red and it hurts me so that I could hardly walk home and I thought perhaps I will die, who knows if I will die? Who will cure me? Will God cure me? Will the señorita cure me? Perhaps the señorita will cure me. I will ask her to stick me with her needle. Will you stick me?"

I took out the vial of penicillin. There were still several cc's left, more than enough for an injection. "Yes," I said, "I will inject you. Rosa, would you boil my needle in your pot?"

"Pava! Bring the small pot. Get some water. How much water, señorita?"

"Just a little in the bottom. No, that's too much."

Pava tipped some of the water into the ashes beside the fire. "Like that, señorita?"

"Yes, like that."

"Blow up the fire, Pava! Hurry!" said Rosa. "The señorita says she will boil her needle. There. The needle, señorita? Will you put it in the pot?"

I put the needle, together with the syringe and forceps, into the pot and began to examine the leg which Pedro stretched toward the fire. It was swollen and inflamed, and pus ran in a little trickle between the sparse black hairs of his leg. The wound looked deep and painful. Here I was again, the doctor. There was no escaping it. But how lucky that I was here at this moment with the necessary equipment! No, it isn't luck. It's God. He's the one who leads you, Margaret Sparhawk. He has not left you yet. The work may look unpromising but remember the promises of God. Life isn't easy for anyone. It doesn't fall into neat patterns. It's up and down, trusting in the dark, walking in the light, joy and sorrow, sunshine and shadow, whate'er befall, Jesus my Savior is my All in All. . . . The clichés tumbled emptily in my mind and I realized that the needle was bouncing in the pot. It had boiled long enough, and I picked up a cornhusk to use as a potholder.

"Ay, Señorita Margarita, it hurts." Pedro clasped his hands under the thick calf and rocked back, shutting his eyes and lifting his face. His hat, which he had not taken off, fell behind him and I saw that his forehead was beaded with sweat. Not, surely, from the heat, I thought. He must be in real pain. Poor Pedro. I looked at the strong bones of his face—high cheeks, a solid jaw, and lines that drew his mouth down and converged around his eyes. He had known plenty of pain in his lifetime. He had expected little else, I mused. Not physical pain, perhaps—I did not know how much of that he had had. But if pain could be defined as the absence of pleasure he had certainly known that. He was only one of the million. A million highland Quichuas living in cold and loneliness and poverty and hopelessness.

God help me to help him. At least to help Pedro, Lord. You haven't let me do much for the rest, but You brought me here today. Why was it I came? Oh, the house. I had forgotten to ask him about that. Well, it would have to wait for another time. Now for the injection. This is the right thing to do, isn't it, Lord? What else? Lynn gave him penicillin before, I gave him those three injections on the days following hers. The leg had healed up nicely then.

"Does it hurt here, Pedro?" I prodded the area around the open sore. It felt hot and tight.

"*Ay*, señorita. *Aylla*. It hurts very much. All around there, that whole part. Hurts, señorita, it hurts."

I picked up the forceps, which had cooled a little by now and lifted the syringe from the water. Holding the syringe in my left hand, I lifted the needle and fitted it onto the syringe. Pava watched intently.

"Why do you cook it, señorita?"

"To kill the little things that make sickness."

"What little things make sickness?"

I knew no Quichua equivalent for germ. "They're little things you can't see. Tiny. Much smaller than fleas. They get inside us and make us sick. I cook the needle so that I won't give your father someone else's sickness."

"In the cooking the little things die?"

"Yes." I found a small bottle of alcohol in my bag and a wad of cotton. Pedro moved over to his bed and lay down, familiar with the procedure.

"Gently, señorita, *gently*."

I swabbed the brown flesh and plunged the needle in deeply, drawing the plunger out a little way first to make sure I had not reached a vein, then pressing it slowly until all the white liquid was emptied from the barrel.

"*Aylla!* It hurts very much."

[223]

"There. That's all." I rinsed the syringe in the pot and began to put the things away again in my bag.

"Aren't you going to put something on my leg?" asked Pedro.

"Oh. I'm sorry. Of course I will." What should I put on it? The leg was so angry-looking, none of my remedies seemed powerful enough to affect it, but I cleaned up the edges of the wound, fearful to clean the inside lest I introduce further infection. Then I shook in a little surgical powder.

"Will that dust cure me, señorita?"

"I hope it will help, Pedro. The injection is stronger. I think the injection will cure you."

I began to wrap the leg with sterile gauze, holding Pedro's foot in my lap. The toes were thick and club-shaped, coated with earth from his fields. They had walked many, many miles over such earth, and over the roads that led to town, over the cobblestones and over the sidewalks. Strong feet, I thought. The feet of a real man. I wrapped slowly and carefully, holding the leg as lightly as I could. God, heal this leg. What if it doesn't heal? Pedro, a cripple? What would his family do?

"It will heal up all right, will it, señorita?" It was Rosa, who had turned from her place at the fire to watch the bandaging, and now looked into my face searchingly. "He won't die?"

I laughed. "Oh, Rosa. Of course he won't die. It is only his leg, just a bad wound, but the needle medicine will help it."

"*Aylla!* What is it that itches?" Pedro suddenly sat up, pulling his foot from my lap. His lips were stretched in a grimace and he began frantically scratching his hips and thighs.

[224]

"It itches, señorita. *Mana pacha*, how it itches! As if there were a thousand fleas biting me. *Aylla!*" His voice rose to a cry and he jumped from the bed and began to dance around the fire, flailing his arms, scratching and digging at his flesh wherever it was exposed, rubbing at the seat of his trousers.

"What is the matter, Pedro?" I asked, suddenly frightened at the violence of his behavior.

"*Taita Dios!* What is the matter with you?" Rosa started from her seat on the ground. "Are you crazy? He's dreaming! He's out of his mind, señorita!"

Pedro threw himself on the bed again, tearing his poncho off and throwing it across the hut. "They are eating me. Father God, they are eating me! Fleas. Lots of fleas. Who will save me? *Aylla*, señorita, who will save me?"

Rosa rubbed his arms and legs vigorously, asking over and over, "What is the matter? What is the matter? Are you dreaming? Are you crazy?"

"Who knows what it is? How it itches! My whole flesh itches. What kind of fleas will they be that can bite like this? *Aylla*, what will become of me?"

"Try bathing him with some hot water, Rosa," I suggested.

"Pava! Hot water! Hurry and heat some water. A lot of water."

Pava jerked a pot out from a corner and dipped water from the huge clay jar that stood in a depression in the earth. She set it on the fire and energetically flapped the reed fan up and down, sticking corncobs and grass into the coals at the same time. "What is the matter with father?" she asked.

"Who knows what has happened to him? *Heat the water!*"

God in heaven, I thought, have I done something to him? What can possibly have caused this? Pedro's arms suddenly stopped flailing and fell along the sides of the bed. His eyes closed and he was mumbling something.

"What are you saying?" Rosa bent over him, beside herself with fear.

"My head spins. Everything goes around."

"Have the fleas stopped biting you?"

"Fleas . . . Around and around my head turns."

"Is this hot enough, Mama?"

Rosa went and dipped a finger in the pot. "I guess it is right. Here. Bring it over here quickly." She sloshed warm water from the pot onto Pedro's face, neck and hands.

"Why do you get me wet? Leave me alone. Leave me . . . My head . . ." His voice trailed off.

"The fleas—the itch. Does it still itch? Does it still itch? Speak!"

Pedro said nothing, but he was not scratching. He lay quiet, his eyes closed, his hands lying limp, with the palms upward, on the sheepskins. Like a flash a word came to my mind from a medical book. Anaphylaxis. Could that be what had happened? O Lord save us and help us—show me what to do, spare Pedro. But it is so rare—reaction to a drug. Fatal unless immediate aggressive treatment is administered. What treatment? What can I do here?

"Pava! Some garlic! Bring some garlic quickly," Rosa shouted.

Pava found a little knot of garlic somewhere in the thatch and gave it to Rosa, who broke it open and rubbed it on Pedro's lips and nostrils. Hardly aggressive, that treatment. What to do? Oh, what, Lord, shall I do? *You* do something. Maybe it's just a temporary setback. Maybe it isn't anaphylaxis at all—one chance in a hundred. Ridiculous of me to get panicky. He's in Your hands, Lord.

[226]

I watched the strong, dark face. The boldly chiseled lips, the line of his eyebrows, the straight, large nose. What a beautiful subject for a bronze bust! No . . . a bronze mask. Death mask. Pedro. Oh, Pedro. Open your eyes.

For a second I thought he read my unspoken plea. There was a movement of his eyelids. I leaned forward in an agony of hope. Yes. The eyes rolled under the lids, but did not open. Then I saw that his lips were parted. They moved futilely for a moment, and then he spoke. Rosa put her ear to his mouth.

"*Chunlla!* Shut up, children! Your father is talking."

"What does he say?" said Pava.

"*Chunlla!*" She was listening, her mouth wide open, eyes staring. Pedro spoke, then, clearly enough for me to hear him.

"Señorita. It is dark. All becomes dark. Señorita."

"Dark, Pedro?"

"Yes. Very dark, like night."

"Can you hear me?" I thought his head nodded.

"Can you hear me, Pedro?" Answer me, Pedro, say yes. Oh, please hear me!

"Yes, señorita. I can hear you. Do you hear me? I said it is dark." He spoke clearly, rationally, and my heart gave a lunge of joy. He probably fainted and is coming to, I thought, and now all will be well. Lord, let it be. Let it be well.

There was the sudden thud of bare feet in the dooryard, the guinea pigs went scuttling off into the corners, the sun that lay in a patch on the floor was blotted by a shadow, and Romero and Jorge came tumbling through the door, choking with laughter, and threw themselves on a pile of skins.

"*Caramba! Chunlla!* Your father is dying! Don't you know your father is dying?" The tension in Rosa's voice made her fairly spit the words. "As if anyone had said to you, *Laugh!* Is one to laugh when a man is dying?"

I could see the convulsed faces of the two small boys in the firelight. The light in the flashing black eyes and on the white teeth was extinguished in an instant.

"Dying? Father is dying?" said Romero.

"Dying, I said! Don't you see?"

"What happened?"

"Shut up!"

"No, Rosa. Don't say he is dying," I pleaded. This was an expression I had never been able to accept. The Quichua term for anything other than perfect health was "dying." For them, it was the first possibility. For me, it was the last, and I refused to accept it now. Pedro would not be dying.

"As if he will live!" The scorn in Rosa's voice withered me. "Can't you *see* he is dying, señorita? You put that needle into him; you killed him."

Lord God, Father of us all, if You've never heard me pray before, hear me now. Hear what she says. Lord, for the honor of Your name, show what You can do. Save him, Lord, save him.

A little skinny rooster hopped to the doorsill, crowing thinly. Romero heaved a corncob in his direction and he fluttered off. There was no sound in the house now, except Pedro's faint breathing. The rest of us hardly dared to breathe, waiting.

Pedro began to retch, his chest rising, his belly contracting in great tormented spasms. I could see the tendons in his neck stretch and ripple, a knot rose and fell under the weathered skin, and he gagged uncontrollably.

"He will vomit! Pava! Give me the pot!"

Rosa held Pedro's head over the pot while the retching went on and on, violent, body-racking sounds, until it seemed that his entrails must come forth from his throat, but nothing came. His back arched and writhed and his fingers dug into the sheepskins. Lord, quiet him. Deliver him.

The paroxysms ceased then, and Rosa let his head fall back on the bed. The sleeve of her blouse was wet with his perspiration.

"Señorita! What will become of us? He is going to die! He is dying! Señorita! You said you would make him well! Saying, I will cure him, you gave him the needle. Now he will die."

Jorge began to cry loudly. Romero pushed an elbow into his face. "Shut up!"

"Why should he shut up? His father is dying. He is dying, my husband is dying, what will become of us all?" Rosa put both hands on top of her head and began to rock, her words sliding into the singsong death wail I had heard before.

> "Here you stood alive this morning,
> Beside the fire.
> Here you drank the *mazamorra* that I handed to you,
> Drank it all,
> Not thinking to yourself, Today I will die.
> He is alive, we thought,
> And this is how you die on us.
> My husband, my little husband!
> Who will take care of me?
> Who will work?
> What will become of us, my husband?"

You will find another, Rosa. There are always men ready to take a widow. It will be hard for a time, I know. But he is not going to die! God spare him! O Lord, spare him, for Christ's sake! What will become of Rosa? Of

[229]

Rosa? What, Lord God, will become of *Your work?* You started all this, Lord. It wasn't I. You led me here. You answered prayers and gave me Pedro—he is the only one You have given me, Lord, remember that. O Lord, remember that. There is no one else.

No. I must trust Him for healing now. He raised the dead. He healed all kinds of sickness. What is the line from the hymn? . . . "Thy touch hath still its ancient power."

"Rosa, would you like to pray to God that He will help Pedro?"

"To God?" Rosa took her hands from her head and turned her streaming face to me, bewildered.

"Yes, to my God—to the God Pedro believes in."

"Pray, señorita, if you want to. You pray."

"Come here, children, and we will pray," I said. Pava, Jorge and Romero came and squatted in a circle by the fire. The three-year-old had fallen asleep in the shadows. Each child watched me carefully to ascertain the proper procedure. I closed my eyes, and Romero whispered loudly, "Shut your eyes."

"Our Father God, You can do anything You want. We know that You love Pedro, and that if You want to You can make him well. Don't let him die, Lord, please don't let him die. He has believed in You and has served You and You know how he has helped with the translation of Your word. In order that he may go on serving You, Father God, cause him to live. For the glory of Your name, cause him to live. And—because we love him, Lord, cause him to live. In the name of Jesus we pray, Amen."

Pava, who had heard Pedro pray on one or two occasions, said, "Amen."

From the bed behind us we could hear a soft wheeze. Pedro lay very still, breathing shallowly with a sound like a small bellows, his mouth slightly open, the whites of his eyes showing a thin line beneath the lids. Rosa kept feeding corncobs and grass into the fire, as though by sustaining the flame she would prolong the life that flickered on the bed beside her. Carefully, almost stealthily, she chose a bit of straw and put it in place, blowing softly as she did so, watching till the little tongue of fire rose.

What had the medical book said about the symptoms of a drug reaction? I tried to sift my memory for the details. Had it said something about coma or collapse? I could not recall a description of the retching or this wheezing I heard now. Perhaps my diagnosis was mistaken. Lord, let me be mistaken. Perhaps he is delirious from fever, caused by the inflammation. The penicillin has not yet had time to start working. Maybe in a little while . . .

Immediate aggressive treatment. Take him to Indi Urcu? There's no hospital there. The clinic? They wouldn't know anything. Wouldn't admit him, probably, since he's an Indian. Still, we could try. Try? How? There was no one to carry him. There wasn't a man for a mile or so. It's too long a journey anyway. He wouldn't survive the journey. Would he, Lord? Should I try to find someone? No, it's nonsense. Be still and pray. You've done enough damage. I? Was it I who did the damage? My God! I was trying to help him. I was trying to *help* him.

"Pava!" It was Pedro's voice; it was a shout. We jumped with the shock. He was sitting up, blindly fumbling with the sheepskins around him, as though searching for something. "Pava! Get my poncho. My poncho, quickly, Pava. They are coming!"

Pava snatched the poncho from the floor and thrust it toward her father. He opened his eyes, and they moved back and forth wildly, seeing none of us, filled with fear.

[231]

He made a movement with his legs, as though to climb off the bed, then turned suddenly and looked behind him. His fingers clutched the skins. "Pava! Señorita! Father God!"

"Pedro." I spoke his name quietly, hoping to arrest his fear. What did he fear? Was he beside himself? Did he know he was dying? Lord, You are our Refuge. Comfort him. Quiet him.

Rosa was staring at him, while at the same time she beat the reed fan up and down with great fervor, causing the fire to flame high for a few moments. Pedro continued to turn and grasp, trying desperately to focus his eyes on something that was not there. Then, with a groan, he collapsed onto the bed again. Rosa's hand let go of the fan, and she gave herself up to weeping, throwing her hands to her head and then clawing at Pedro's arm, rocking and wailing. Once she rubbed the garlic clove on his lips and went back again to renewed hopelessness, seeing that it did not revive him.

It occurred to me to take Pedro's pulse. I reached for his left hand, thrown far on the other side of the bed. It was cold and limp and felt like dry leather in my hand. Oh Pedro, don't die on us. This can't be the time to die.

I pressed my fingertips to the soft side of his wrist. At last I felt a light throb, much too light, much too weak, for a man. I was unsure for a moment whether I had really felt a throb. Yes, there it was again, the tiny signal that the heart still labored.

"What is it, señorita?" Rosa asked, pausing in her wail when she saw me lift the arm.

"His heart, Rosa. I can feel his heart beat."

"There?"

"Yes."

"How is it? Is he alive?"

"Yes." Still alive. God save him. Save him, Lord. Keep the heart beating. Yes, like that. Still going.

The pulse was thready and I thought every minute that I was only imagining that it beat. No, there it was. Tick . . . tick, tick . . . Giver and Sustainer of Life, give him life today, sustain Pedro's life, Lord. You are the doer of all that's been done through him so far. You raised him from eternal death to eternal life, brought him from heathen darkness to Your blazing light. Gave me a soul for the Kingdom, an earnest of the inheritance You would grant me among this tribe, a product of grace. My product, too, Lord, the fruit of all my work here. Spare him. Spare him. Spare him.

I found that I had taken up, in my mind, the rhythm of Rosa's death wail. My prayer was being chanted to the tune of her cry, "He's dying, he's dying, he's dying." Her voice soared again to the narrative, recalling what Pedro did for the family, how he went to work in the morning, how he was unaware of his approaching death. Gradually it sank to the reiteration of her own despair, what would become of her, what would become of the children? And then to the simple declaration of the reality, "He's dying, he's dying, he's dying."

The fire had dwindled to a few embers that waved and blinked. The sun by this time had disappeared and the chickens began to come into the hut to roost for the night. Jorge amused himself by throwing bits of straw and twigs at them, making them cluck and fluff their feathers as they settled themselves on the pole. The baby began to cry, making Rosa halt abruptly in her dirge. She picked him up from his hammock, gave him the breast and settled again on the floor beside Pedro, taking up once more the keening lament.

[233]

Pava and Romero sat hushed in the gathering dark. Their father was dying. The one on whom everything, life itself, depended. Their bulwark against hunger and nakedness and the white man. How much did they comprehend of this?

Now and again Pedro's hands twitched. His head had fallen back at a grotesque angle and I tried to rearrange it. Strange, how heavy it was in my hands. I moved it a little, feeling the weight. Dear Pedro. What will I do? *What will I do?*

Find the pulse again. See if it's working. Tick . . . Is that it? No . . . That? . . . Yes—no . . . Tick. There it is! One tiny throb. I was sure I felt it. Yes, he is alive—his eyes are opening.

Pedro's head fell again into the position from which I had moved it, his eyelids parted a little, his jaw worked back and forth for a few seconds. Then he gave a deep sigh and was still.

"Rosa," I said.

She jerked her head around and looked me full in the eyes, a wild animal look, full of terror and hatred. Then she leaped up from the floor and threw herself shrieking onto her husband's body. The baby was still held in one arm, and he, too, began to shriek. Pava, Jorge and Romero crowded to the mound of skins where their dead father lay, their eyes wide and glittering in the feeble firelight.

21

IT WAS so dark by this time I could hardly see the trail, but I must hurry. I was almost running, putting my feet down recklessly and wrenching my ankles as I tripped on the broken clods of clay. It had never seemed such a long way home. I strained toward the town, pulling it toward me, running and running, trying to push the mountain away behind, pushing the little mud hut back and back.

"Follow the Shepherd, Margaret. He knows the way."

It was too late now. My eyes strained through the dark, trying to light the lamps of the town somewhere there below me. Where was the trail? The turn onto the cobblestone road? Was it here? Hurry.

Somewhere nearby I heard the bleat of a sheep. I was out of breath and something about the feel of the road beneath my feet was not quite familiar. Every rut and rock was known to me on the usual route. I had better stop. But there isn't time. There's no time to stop. The animal look, the wild shriek, the implacable corpse—were they actually following me? No. They were back in the hut, far up the mountain now. Stop. You've lost your way.

I stood still on the trail and tried to listen, but found that I was panting and my legs were trembling and it took a minute before I could hear the silence around me. The night was still and frigid and the stars, like fearsome watchers, hovered close above me. I should by this time have reached the turn onto my road, but somewhere I had missed it. A sheep cried again—a forsaken, human cry— and I remembered the place where the sheep lived. I was not far from my road. I knew now which way to turn. Hurry. Better start running again.

The light of the stars was not enough to enable me to see anything that I recognized, but to my right, like a jagged orange tear in the fabric of the dark, a fire glowed on the hills. It must be far away, I decided, so it must be to the east. I was going north, then, where I wanted to go. Some Indian must be burning his pasture land. The fire was like a thin dragon, trembling and creeping across the night.

I started to walk again, quickly, and in a few moments I heard a dog bark, then I saw a light, then two lights, and the trail dropped to the cobblestone road. I ran as fast as I could. Perhaps there would still be time.

Time for what? I reached my gate, jerked at the latch and fumbled with it in the dark, wanting to tear it from its screws. It came open, and I ran to the door, but my hands were shaking so that the key would not fit into the lock.

"Fear thou not; for I am with thee: be not dismayed; for I am thy God." Still with me? Still my God? No. It was too late. There. The key turned, the door opened, and I rushed into the house, turned on all the lights, and sank down by the table.

Everything was exactly as I had left it. The rag rug on the floor, the awkward chairs that had long since lost their awkwardness in my eyes, the flowered tablecloth and the teapot, the Swiss clock. But the clock had stopped. Had I forgotten to wind it, or had there actually been, as I seemed to sense, some cosmic change that marked the end of something? I picked up the clock, wound it and shook it, then listened. It was not ticking. Good, I thought, and set it down on the table. That gives me time, then. Time to begin again, slowly, carefully, to sort things out.

Surely there is a way to make it come right. This can't be it. It isn't finished yet. Go back and do it the other way this time. Do it right. For God's sake, *do it right* this time.

Was it the medicine? Would streptomycin have worked? No, no. You have to go back much farther than that. It was something else. There must have been a call that you didn't hear—or was it that you disobeyed? A dozen accusations confronted me. No. I refuse to capitulate. How could I have failed to hear the call that was meant for me? What kind of a shepherd would allow that? No one had ever listened more intently, praying, beseeching, entreating God to guide, to show the way. The call had come, the way had opened, the work had begun. Had I disobeyed? *Had* I? Where could it have been? Is God through with me now, is He saying, "Get out"? The Indians are through with me. Rosa had stabbed me with her hatred.

These four walls—they are still here. My home. My quiet place to come back to after visiting the Indians. The house is still here. They can't reach me here. Nobody can reach me here. But God can. Where is the refuge from Him? I was going to sacrifice this home for You! What of the sacrifices I have already made—did You toy with them? O ineffable, sardonic God who toys with our sacrifices and smashes to earth the humble, hopeful altars we have built for a place to put Your name! Do You mock

[237]

me? Why did You let him die? Why did You let me kill him? O God! I came to bring him life—*Your* life—and I destroyed him in Your name.

A donkey clopped by on the road outside and I could hear the sound of a whip and an Indian voice. Then there was silence. I looked at the Bible on the table in front of me and started to pick it up. My hand dropped again. I could not find answers there any more. Nothing had worked for me as I had thought it would work. God had nothing to say to me now. Where was He, anyway?

The question, which in my mind was tantamount to declaring myself an atheist, found me sitting there at the table waiting for an answer. Who would answer? Who, if not God Himself? Well, I would wait for Him. Perhaps He would strike me dead. No, that is unlikely. He could hardly bother with me to that extent now. Probably He has forgotten. Or He could answer me out of the whirl-wind, vindicate Himself, explain. No, I have probably gone too far astray ever to hear Him again.

What shall I do now? Make some tea. Do something. See if anything works—does water boil as before? This silence! How can things be the same? How can the house stand so smugly as it stood this morning, nothing changed, every-thing in its place, quiet, neat, oblivious? Only the clock has stopped.

The beginning and the end. I have come to the end of my work. God's work, I thought it was—I came here for Him. I ventured to believe He had given it to me to do, and I staked my life on it. I entered into it in faith and now . . . the end. *And omega.* God! My God!

"Señorita!" I jumped in my chair. It was Pava outside the door. "Señorita Margarita!"

I stumbled to the door and opened it. "Pava!"

"Mama says have you any candles to give us for the wake for Father?"

Candles. A wake for Father. My mind teetered to find its balance again, confronted with two specifics. Did I have any candles?

"Yes, Pava, I think I have. Come in. I will look for them." I found some candles in the kitchen cupboard and brought them out. As though my heart had been hit with a hammer, I realized that had it not been for me they would not have needed candles. Pedro would not have been dead.

"Well, good night, señorita," said Pava. "May God pay you." She turned to go.

"Good night, Pava." I opened the door for her, and saw that Romero was waiting in the dark. She would not have to go home alone. I started to close the door and Romero called, "Señorita."

"What is it, Romero?"

"Señorita—we are having a wake and Mama wanted to . . . Mama said would you come and sit with us?"

Yes, I thought. I can do that. I can go and sit with them.

IF I had said no to Romero and Pava, and had not gone to their father's wake, I would probably have forsaken my place among the Indians of the highland, and perhaps my place as a missionary anywhere at all. But then I do not really know. The decision was not one which I weighed carefully. The children came and brought their request, and I went with them. It seems to me now that the decision was right, and that it was indeed the voice of God, still and small, that said, "And omega." Perhaps He would have borne with me even if I had said no, and have brought me by another way. He is indeed of great mercy. Only I know that I was glad to have been at the wake, and I am glad to be here in my house in Indi Urcu.

The sun shines today, as you know that it nearly always does in the mornings, and the great mountain Chimborazo shines with it, lifting its gleaming peak toward heaven, reminding me that the strength of the hills is His also.

The only light at the wake came from the two candles we brought. One was placed at Pedro's head, one at his feet, and Rosa bent over him in the yellow circle, her black hair falling across his face, and wailed the death wail until the cocks began to crow at dawn. People came from all over the mountain, packing themselves into the stuffy little room (the candles flickered for lack of oxygen), crying for a little while, talking, sitting stolidly in the gloom until another mourner arrived, when it was necessary briefly to renew the wailing. Rosa uncovered the face of the corpse when a relative came, and each time she did so the features looked a trifle younger and sharper, the deep tea color of his skin gradually paler. I found myself spellbound by the sight of that face, which had registered nothing when Pedro first met me, then, as time had passed, had shown shy friendliness, trust, interest, eagerness, joy—would it not change now, would not a single tiniest muscle twitch, an eyelash fall? Rosa covered the face again, more tenderly than I had seen her do anything, and then raised her arms to her head once more and rocked and chanted. And then when the cocks had crowed and darkness was driven over the far eastern hills the mourners got up one by one, straightened their ponchos and their skirts, and left the house, filing off over the cracked fields to their work. A few of the men stayed to wait for the coffin which had been sent for from the town. They put the body in it, there was another night of watching, and on the morning of the second day I saw the long file moving toward the village, four men carrying the wooden coffin on their shoulders. I went with them, too, to the Indian section of the little cemetery. The relatives had hired a few professional mourners—poor white people who knew the prayers that had to be said and possessed rosaries which they agreed to use in exchange for some corn and *chicha*.

Pava stood quietly by the open grave, a single ray of sunlight falling across her cheekbones under the wide, upturned brim of her felt hat. As the ropes let the coffin gently into the earth I saw the glitter of tears on her lashes.

When the earth was thrown onto the coffin and stamped down, she wrapped her shawl tightly around her arm, and pushed her nose into the crook of her elbow, her shoulders heaving with sobs. Rosa wept openly, as was expected of her at the grave, and when it was over she took her children home in silence, there to take up what God had left her of life.

I wonder whether I will ever live in an Indian house. Even here in Indi Urcu the people come casually, now and then, to visit me. I go to visit them and they talk as freely or they are as silent as ever. If they talk, they often speak of Pedro's death and my part in it. There is no conspiracy of silence between us on that subject. If they are silent it is not a different silence from before. Some are as hostile and suspicious as they have ever been but not, I think, more so; some are slowly losing their reticence, like Manuela, who asked me if her small relatives could join Pedro's children in the reading classes. I still have the classes. Of course they are not formal. The children come to my house now, when they feel like coming, and we spread out the books on the tiny verandah or, if the group is too large, in the fenced enclosure. Some of them make astonishing strides and then abruptly stop coming. Others, without the slightest flagging of hope and enthusiasm, learn nothing at all, though they come week after week. Perhaps the reading classes will come to an end. God knows about that. As for the translation of the Bible, of course, I cannot go ahead without an informant. God knew about that when Pedro died. I do not write prayer letters any more, for I have nothing to say about my work. It seemed, on the night of Pedro's death, as though *Finis* were written below all I had done. Now, in the clear light of day, I see that I was in part correct. God, if He was merely my accomplice, had betrayed me. If, on the other hand, He was God, He had freed me.

I find that I can no longer arrange my life in an orderly succession of projects with realizable goals and demonstrable effects. I cannot designate this activity as "useful" and that one as "useless," for often the categories are reversed and even more often I am at a loss to apply either label, for the work, in the end, as well as the labeling, is God's.

One day a few weeks ago I went down to the village graveyard again to visit Pedro's grave. The paper flowers that had been put there had faded and were laden with dust. The mound of earth had sunk a little. But at the head of the grave someone had put up a flimsy wooden cross, painted white, and had written in pencil the name PEDRO CHIMBU, and the date of his death.

Nothing else had changed. The sky was vast and blue above me, the mountains calm around me. There was no sound except that of a few sheep beyond the mud wall, and a faint piping as someone—it sounded like a child—went by on the road, playing on his panpipes.

It was as it should be. I found myself alone—Rosa was not here, but carrying out her own work at home; the MacDonalds, Lynn, my colleagues in many places had also their appointed tasks for which they would individually give account; those who prayed for me at home might at this moment be praying, and He to whom the prayers were addressed would know what answer to give. For my part, I was left alone before God—indeed, it seemed to me this morning that for the first time in my life I stood in direct relation to Him as Moses stood when he beheld the burning bush. For me, however, it was no such dramatic vision. There were before me only the dry mound of earth and the pitiful little cross with its penciled legend. What was it about that cross that cleared the way to God? I think it was this: I saw for the first time my own identity in its true perspective. Once I had envisioned Pedro, highland Indian, Christian, translator of the Bible, soldier of the Cross—because I, Margaret Sparhawk, had come. He was my project, he was the star in my crown. But here was another cross, with a name and a date, to mark where a dead man lay—because I, Margaret Sparhawk, had come.

And God? What of Him? "I am with thee," He had said. With me in *this?* He had allowed Pedro to die, or—and I could not then nor can I today deny the possibility—He had perhaps caused me to destroy him. And does He now, I asked myself there at the graveside, ask me to worship Him?

I lay down on the grass and saw that high above me a condor circled, looking down on the tops of the frosted peaks, on the lakes and the serene valley. The child went by the gate once more, piping softly.